the TEENAGE GUY'S SURVIVAL GUIDE ⟶

the TEENAGE GUY'S SURVIVAL GUIDE →

The real deal on GOING OUT, GROWING UP, and OTHER GUY STUFF

by Jeremy DALDRY

Little, Brown and Company

New York Boston

Little, Brown and Company
Hachette Book Group
1290 Avenue of the Americas, New York, NY 10104
Visit us at LBYR.com

Originally published in 1999 by Piccadilly Press in Great Britain
First U.S. Edition: May 1999
Revised Edition: April 2018

Little, Brown and Company is a division of Hachette Book Group, Inc.
The Little, Brown name and logo are trademarks of Hachette Book Group, Inc.

The publisher is not responsible for websites (or their content) that are not owned by the publisher.

Library of Congress Cataloging-in-Publication Data
Names: Daldry, Jeremy, 1969– author. | Daldry, Jeremy, 1969– Boys behaving badly.
Title: The teenage guy's survival guide : the real deal on going out, growing up, and other guy stuff / Jeremy Daldry.
Description: Revised edition. | New York : Little, Brown Books for Young Readers, 2018. | Revised edition of the author's The teenage guy's survival guide, 1999.
Identifiers: LCCN 2017036938| ISBN 9780316561433 (paperback) | ISBN 9780316561426 (hardcover) | ISBN 9780316561419 (ebook)
Subjects: LCSH: Teenage boys—United States—Juvenile literature. | Adolescence—Juvenile literature. | Puberty—Juvenile literature. | Interpersonal relations in adolescence—Juvenile literature. | CYAC: Teenage boys. | Puberty. | Sex instruction for boys.
Classification: LCC HQ797 .D35 2018 | DDC 305.235/10973—dc23
LC record available at https://lccn.loc.gov/2017036938

ISBNs: 978-0-316-56142-6 (hardcover), 978-0-316-56143-3 (pbk.), 978-0-316-56141-9 (ebook)

Printed in the United States of America

LSC-C

Hardcover: 10 9 8 7 6 5 4 3 2 1
Paperback: 10 9 8 7 6 5 4 3 2 1

D...Everything begins and ends with you.
For holding my hand, for loving me, for being my friend.
For making something that was incomplete whole again.

CONTENTS

Facial Hair

Pimples, Zits, Eruptions

Greasy Hair

Being Stinky

Your Voice

CHAPTER THREE

CHAPTER FOUR

WHAT'S THIS BOOK ALL ABOUT, ANYWAY?

Arrrrrrgh! What? Where? When? Who?

WHAT'S HAPPENING TO ME?

Take a deep breath. Relax. Don't panic.

It's called being a **teenager**.

And it's perfectly normal.

And besides, that's why you (or someone else) bought this *excellent*, and **PRETTY FUNNY**, book—to help answer those pesky questions and offer you a user's guide to being a teenage guy.

So what's this book all about, then?

Literally, everything.

Dates, kissing, dumping, being dumped, broken hearts, crushes, shaving, zits, greasy hair, being stinky, masturbation, wet dreams, success, failure, depression, confidence, listening, talking, drinking, drugs, peer pressure, bullying, fighting, parents, clothes, friends, money, the Internet, social media, "anti-social" media.

Oh, and did I mention dates?

Cool!

CHAPTER ONE

SURVIVING LOVE AND SEX

LIKING GIRLS

Girls...They are just great. In fact, look up the word *great* in the dictionary and there will be a picture of a GIRL. They are that good.

We love them.

But that doesn't stop girls from being the cause of more heartache, confusion, and sleepless nights than almost anything else.

They might be wonderful—but they are also weird. All that giggling over the latest Snapchat filter, lip-synching to pop songs, and spending hours doing their nails and hair. What is that all about? I mean...really, **WHAT IS THAT ALL ABOUT?**

And as for trying to talk to them...

It's been scientifically proven that when any straight guy gets within two feet of a girl, she gives off a mysterious aura that turns that guy into a jabbering wreck who can't string two words together.

Ywohtz hibby brb?

It's proven. It's science. Strange but true.

But, despite all of this, you still want to talk to them.

You want to be close to them.

You want to hold their hands,

and go out on dates with them.

And kiss them, and cuddle them,

and kiss them, and kiss them some more.

And bingo, there is the first **BIG** problem: asking a girl out on a date.

Even when it's totally obvious that a girl has a huge crush on you, even if all her friends are looking at you both and going "I SHIP them so HARD," even if every time she looks at you there are literally hearts shooting out of her eyes and a rainbow coming out of her mouth...

Even if all of THIS is happening...why do you find it so hard to just go up and ask her out?

I'll tell you why.

Because you're scared of being rejected, or of the girl in question telling her friends, who will all laugh at you.

But it shouldn't be scary, because, let's face it: You probably know when a girl wants to be asked out.

No, you do, really.

Does she wear a T-shirt that says "Ask me out"?

You just need to look out for the little signs that mean a girl could like you (and I'm not talking about hearts and rainbows shooting out of her head).

Like?

Well, when you talk to her:

- *She blushes, or she starts to play with her hair.*
- *She smiles when she sees you coming and "accidentally" touches you on the hand or leg when you leave.*
- *She laughs at your lame jokes, asks lots of questions about you, and then listens really closely to whatever you've got to say.*

But wait a minute. What is so wrong with a *girl* asking one of us *guys* to a party or to the movies?

Please ask me OUT!

There is no rule that says girls can't ask boys out. They should. It makes us feel wanted and means that for once we guys don't have to go through the pre-asking-out-on-a-date **hell**.

So if there are any GIRLS reading this book, take a hint: **Ask more boys out. WE LIKE IT!**

That is a VERY good HINT!

But before we attack the hows, whys, and wherefores of what to do on your red-hot date, it's worth talking about the fact that you might not think about, crush on, or love girls the way other people do. There are other *types* of people to like, and other *ways* to like those people.

Liking Guys

First of all, all this stuff holds true if the person you want to date is a girl or a guy. Talking to a crush—no matter what their plumbing—can be nerve-racking.

And despite what you might think, **it isn't weird or abnormal** to develop huge crushes on, or even be sexually attracted to, members of the same sex.

It's very common. Does it mean you're gay? It might, or it might not.

> As long as you've got someone to hug and squeeze, what does it matter?

Sometimes people take crushes a little further and experiment physically with members of the same sex. Again, there is nothing wrong with that. Lots of people experiment with their sexuality.

In fact, it's estimated that ONE OUT OF EVERY THREE BOYS and ONE OUT OF EVERY FIVE GIRLS have been with members of the same sex.

Are you freaked out by that?

> No...are you?

You shouldn't be. It's completely normal.

Just because you experiment, it doesn't automatically mean you are gay.

And in the same way that having a crush on another guy doesn't mean that you *are* gay, dating a girl doesn't necessarily mean that you *aren't* gay.

Some guys settle down and get married to a woman, have

children, and then realize that they prefer guys. There are no rules about how you feel or who you should like.

EVERYTHING IS NORMAL.

Everything? What about dancing around in your underwear with a frozen chicken on your head while juggling avocados? Is that normal?

And if you do decide you prefer other guys to girls, there's no problem with that. It's estimated that at least one in ten people are gay.

Just because you find other guys sexually attractive, it doesn't mean that you are weird or a pervert.

Gay guys are the same as straight guys.

They just like other men.

They don't watch you in the shower.

They don't try to hit on every guy they talk to.

They don't listen to only Lady Gaga.

They don't cry at the drop of a hat.

They don't all have unhealthily close relationships with their mothers.

Gay men are teachers, rock stars, government officials, lawyers, policemen, comedians, and bus drivers. They live their lives the same as any other guy. No one should feel isolated or alone because of who he finds attractive.

If you think you might be gay because you've got a crush on another guy and:

- *you feel confused,*
- *you think your parents wouldn't understand,*
- *or you feel that you are the only gay guy in the world...*

TALK TO SOMEONE ABOUT IT.

Oh, yeah, right. Like who?

Your brother, sister, friends, other family members. People who know and love you. Or if you find it easier to talk to someone in confidence or anonymously, then you could try your doctor, school guidance counselor, or coach, or any of the hotlines listed in the resources section at the end of this book.

The world has space for all kinds of love...guy and girl, guy and guy, girl and girl. One of the best things about being a teenager is that, if you want to, you can experiment (safely) with different kinds of relationships and find the one that is right for you.

Liking Both

Some guys have always known that they prefer guys. Some guys try girls and then decide they prefer guys after all. Some guys like both guys and girls, with no preference at all. They're bisexual.

This is also sometimes called being pansexual. Not gay, not straight, not bi...just "them." They don't limit their attraction to any one biological sex, or gender identity. Billie Joe Armstrong from Green Day, actor Ezra Miller, and Miley Cyrus have all said that is how they think of themselves. For some reason it's still more common for a woman to come out and discuss her sexuality publicly and for it to be viewed as "no biggie" than for a man to do it—which isn't really fair—but that doesn't mean that lots of guys aren't feeling this way. And if you're one of them—don't sweat it.

Born One / Being the Other

There is a difference between our **sex**—the stuff between our legs and the chromosomes that we are born with—and our **gender**—how we feel, how we see ourselves, and how the world sees us. They are two different things: one biological, one more personal. For most people, whether they are gay or straight, their sex and their gender are the same. Born a guy, sees himself as a guy. But for some people it doesn't quite work like that. You might be born male but see yourself as female. Or vice versa. Some people may choose to dress and present themselves as the gender they feel they are inside. They may want to live their lives like that, or even have surgery to match their sex and gender permanently.

This is called being **transgender,** or **trans,** and is more common than you think.

In fact, in the USA there are forty gender clinics working exclusively with children and adolescents, and the UK's main child gender clinic has seen the number of people they are helping increase by 1000 percent in the last five years. It is NOT uncommon. Check out Jazz Jennings or Gigi Gorgeous on YouTube.

If that's how you feel, you've probably felt it all your life, because being trans isn't a choice—it's just who you are, like having brown eyes or brown hair.

> Wait a minute...I have brown eyes AND brown hair!

And if that *is* how you feel, don't be afraid to seek guidance. There are resources at the end of this book that can help.

If you aren't transgender yourself, but a kid at school comes out as trans, just take a second to think how scary that might be for them and how brave they are to embrace being themselves....Cut them some slack. A smile won't kill you and, heads up, it won't mean they will instantly hit on you—you aren't **that** much of a stud.

Live and let live. Love and let love—that's what I say!

Always remember that **sexuality and gender aren't switches that go on or off,** gay, straight, or trans. It's more like a slide that will eventually land somewhere between gay and straight but may be closer to one than the other. Being confused about your sexuality or gender can be, well...very confusing. It can also be frightening, isolating, and scary. Don't let it be. There are lots of resources that can help.

ASKING SOMEONE OUT

Here's a big tip—supposedly surefire lines like:

"Baby, it's your lucky day!"

"What's a beautiful girl like you doing in a place like this?"

Or:

"Hey, gorgeous, where have you been all my life?"

will only guarantee that you end up spending an awful lot of time ALONE. Girls (and guys!) might want to be asked out, but they don't want to be insulted.

Hey—those are all my best lines!

So there is nothing to do but take a deep breath, walk up to your crush, and say something like:

"Would you like to go out with me on Saturday night?"

It may not be the most subtle or clever thing to say, but sometimes the direct approach is best.

[HERE'S A SECRET.]

You want to be a little sneaky about it? Don't ask—*suggest* a date.

What's the difference? Well...

"Want to go to the Blind Petunia concert with me?"

That will get you a **YES** or **NO** answer.

Huh?

Which is great if the person says YES and not so great if they say NO.

But if you say:

"I've got a couple of tickets for the Blind Petunia concert. I thought I might give you one."

Then you're not forcing the issue—you're easing into it.

It's subtle, it's cute, and it works.

And it makes you think about what you're going to *do* on your date before you ask.

It's sometimes best, when you ask someone out, to give them a few options, or at least to hint at what you'd like to do on your date. They might be less likely to agree if they don't know what they're in for. It could be anything from alphabetizing your extensive collection of vintage 45s to white-water rafting on the Colorado River.

But you also want to be careful not to plan your date in *too much* detail, or you won't have any flexibility to change your plans. It also might make you come across as a little, you know, weird.

So instead of:

"I thought we could meet at the southwest corner of Main and Oak streets at 1600 hours, inspect the local retail outlets until 1645 hours, and then retire to the moving-picture complex to watch the 1700-hours feature."

you could try:

"If you want, we could meet in town around four and then maybe catch a movie."

Safer still is:

"Want to meet at the mall around four and then decide what to do?"

That will give you the chance to check out what's happening that afternoon and plan a few different things. And you never know, your date might even have a few ideas, too.

Some Basic Asking-Out Hacks

It's NOT the best idea to ask someone out when they're surrounded by friends. Even if they're desperate for you to ask them out, it will be embarrassing if all their friends can overhear. And more important, YOU will feel even worse if the answer is NO.

GET to the point. Don't "ummm" and "uhhh." Don't spend hours leading up to asking someone out. Just say hi, ask your crush how they're doing, and then come out with "If you're free on Saturday night..."

DON'T, don't, don't get a friend to ask for you. That's just so tacky. Remember that you are asking this person out because you want to be with them—no other reason. If you get a friend to do the asking, it looks like you don't really care that much whether the answer is YES or NO, *and* it makes you look like a complete coward. Also, your friend might move in on your date!

Hey, I never thought of that....

And for those of you who really want to go for the safe option, there's always the Social Media Ask-Out—or the **SMAO, as it's known absolutely nowhere, ever.**

WhatsApp, Snapchat, texting, Facebook, Twitter, email—there are a whole host of different electronic ways you can ask someone out on a date—although it's probably good to remember that it's a lot nicer to be asked out in person. It's less like Amazon or eBay is asking you to the movies.

And the e-ask-out is not as safe as you think. While it might be easier to ask someone out on a date via social media, it's also easier for them to say no.

In fact, they don't even have to say no. You could message someone for a date and just get 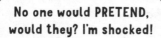 or LOL back—that is, if you get an answer at all. It's easy to miss a message on your phone. Or...to PRETEND TO.

> No one would PRETEND, would they? I'm shocked!

Also, if you **TEXT** that cute girl in Physics 101 about how you like her, want to spend time with her, love the way her hair shimmers in the sunshine, and want to take her on a hot date... she can not only say no, she can also show your text to all her friends, or Retweet it to her fifteen thousand followers, and before you know it you'll be all over the Internet as the **SAD SHIMMERING-HAIR BOY MEME.**

> How did you know that's my nickname? You can call me Hair Boy!

Of course, there's one more option—you can go old-school and give your crush a call on the phone. You know, that thing in your pocket that you use to send texts and listen to music. Some people are more relaxed on the phone. They find it easier to talk. Can't face the girl or guy in the flesh? Call her or him.

But don't BLURT it out or TAKE FOREVER to get to the point. Write a few notes outlining what you want to say before you say it. It's not dorky, and she or he won't be able to tell. Then just pick a good time to call:

- *not too early in the morning,*
- *not too late at night,*
- *not when there's a great show on TV that the person might be watching*

Yeah, like 8:30 PM, when *Generic Teen Drama* starring Brad Meat-Head and Tiffany McBlonde-Brain is on The CW.

and **GO FOR IT.**

But if you do use the phone, and you are calling the family landline, remember to ask to speak to your potential date and say who's calling. People can sound different on the phone, and you don't want this to happen:

"Hi, Madison. I was wondering if you'd like to go to the movies with me on Saturday."

"I think you want to speak to my daughter."

"Oh, sorry. Yes, please."

(CUE silent facepalm.)

Or:

"Hi, this is Madison."

"Hi, Madison. I was just wondering if you'd like to go to the movies with me on Saturday."

"That sounds nice—but who is this?"

Not the best way to start a date.

D'oh!

It's really simple: You want to ask; your date probably wants to be asked. So take your time, get to know the person, smile, be confident, walk up to/call/text/email your crush, and ask them out.

Hello. Umm... wanna go on a date?

What to Do If Your Crush Says No

If the object of your affection does say "Thanks, but no thanks," there is no point pleading, getting down on your knees, or getting all huffy about it. If you ask someone out, they have the right to say no.

Or they might just laugh. Right? Oh...that's just what happens to me, then.

DON'T TAKE IT PERSONALLY,

DON'T GET DEPRESSED BY IT,

DON'T STORM OFF IN A HUFF,

and

DON'T DISRESPECT THE PERSON ALL OVER THE INTERNET WITH BITCHY COMMENTS ON FACEBOOK, INSTAGRAM, AND TWITTER.

It happens to everyone. Sometimes you'll get knocked back, and that can be annoying. Upsetting, even. You can feel angry, and you might also feel a little foolish for having asked in the first place. You might think that everyone knows and that everyone is laughing at you. **NEWS FLASH**—they're not. But even if they are...so what? Get over it. Even the biggest dude in the entire world gets rejected sometimes. It is the right of someone you are asking out to say no, just as it's your right to say no if someone asks you. But if you never ask, you'll never know, and you could be missing out on some really great dates.

No problem—I'll just have a fun Saturday night with the guys. Who needs love anyway?

THE DATE

Okay, so you managed to get up the nerve to ask out the person of your dreams. But now you've actually got to, you know, **GO ON THE DATE.**

What?

   How?

      Where?

         When?

            Argggghh!!!

Don't panic. Take a deep breath. Chill out.

Landing on the moon might seem simple compared to planning a good first date. But don't worry, because it's really easy.

Yeah, right!

And remember, you're not the only one who's freaking out about the whole thing. Your crush will almost certainly be going through exactly the same stomach-turning, last-minute panic.

What to Wear

Everyone thinks it's just girls who spend all day preparing for dates. No way!

We've all done it: sat there trying to decide what to wear, spent so long in the bathroom that your mom comes and knocks on the door and says if you don't stop whatever you're doing you'll go blind, and even stolen some of your dad's aftershave so you smell like a love god.

I've never done that!

So let's start with:

What NOT to Wear

There is no point borrowing your brother's latest club clothes, because if you get as far as a second date, your potential bae might expect you to wear something equally hip. Also, if you "borrow" something from your older brother without asking him, you might have to go on your date minus the hip outfit but plus a black eye.

Don't buy something new. If you blow all your cash on a new outfit and then you're dressed like a loser the next time you see your date, you'll look dumb.

> Dirty T-shirt, four weeks old; torn-up jeans; old sneakers with holes in the toes—how much cooler can you get?

four-week-old shirt →

Don't wear a tie. I mean, come on, a tie? You're not going to your cousin's wedding.*

ripped → jeans

old → sneakers

* Unless, of course, your date is at your cousin's wedding. But really, who takes a date to a wedding?

Good Things to Wear

You want to look like you care—like you've made an effort to look good for your date.

But you should also always wear something that makes you feel comfortable. Studly, scruffy, whatever...as long as it's **YOU,** it really shouldn't matter. Remember, she's going on a date with **YOU,** not with your wardrobe.

> She better not be—my wardrobe is going steady with my nightstand.

Clean would be good. Something that's been sitting on your bedroom floor since first grade and smells of festering jockstrap might not make the kind of impression you are looking for.

And while we're on the subject of what to wear and what not to wear (or smell like), let's talk about cologne.

An entire can of Axe down your boxers does NOT smell good. It will also hurt like crazy, so don't do it.

Ouch, ouch! Too late!

Girls like you to smell nice, so wash your feet—go crazy, wash your hair—but they don't like you to smell like the perfume counter at Macy's. Remember, a little goes a long way.

How to Behave on the Date

So, you smell nice, you look cool, everything is great. Let's talk about the date itself.

You might know this person really well—they might be your best friend—but you've never been on a date with them before. And dates are different. Don't ask me why—they just are. You've asked someone out

TO BE WITH YOU.
ALONE.
BECAUSE YOU LIKE THEM.

Oh, my God—now what?

But remember: You have asked someone out on a date, and they have said **YES.** Relax.

They want to be there.

They want to be with you.

They must like you at least a little.

Not a bad place to start.

The Number One Golden Rule: First impressions count.

I do a great Donald Duck—quack, quack, flap, flap. That kind of impression?

Before You Panic, Here Is a
HANDY 7-POINT CHEAT SHEET FOR YOUR FIRST DATE.*

* This IS NOT a foolproof guide, but it's a start. Probably best to read it BEFORE you go on the date rather than taking it with you. That would make you seem a little weird, and take it from me: WEIRD + DATE does not = SECOND DATE.

1. Before the date.

Your phone CAN be your best friend. A couple of hours before you're supposed to meet (or the evening before, if you're meeting in the morning), send a quick text to see if your date is still able to make it.

Something like...

> YOU: still up for our date tmrw? C u around 4pm @ the mall! Looking forward to it

> DATE: C U there x

...is good.

But...

> YOU: Can you please confirm that you are still happy to attend our social meeting at the prearranged time and place to engage in some enjoyable interaction?

> DATE: Ummm ..... ☹

...is less so.

Also, one text, maybe two, is all it takes. Your date will not want to be text-bombed with dozens and dozens of messages.

Okay...so it's all set. You've confirmed by text, you're showered, you're dressed, you're smelling and looking FINE. Time to move on to the date itself.

2. Be on time.

You've asked someone out and it will not go over well if you're late.

BUT WHAT IF THE PERSON YOU HAVE ASKED OUT IS LATE?

Well, it's polite to wait a little while. You never know—he or she might have been held up or missed their bus.

BUT HOW LONG SHOULD YOU WAIT? AND WHAT SHOULD YOU DO WHILE YOU ARE WAITING?

Twenty minutes is about the minimum you should wait—although if you really like the person, you might find yourself hanging around for at least an hour.

An hour! You've got to be kidding me!

There is nothing worse than waiting on a street corner for someone and feeling like everyone knows you're waiting on a street corner for someone. After about twenty minutes you could send a text to see if your date is stuck somewhere or delayed. But remember what we said about one or two texts **ONLY**. If your date is out of cell reception and then sees **15 TEXTS,** 6 missed calls, 5 Facebook messages, and 4 emails all from you, they might just turn around and go home. **BANG... END OF DATE.**

It's usually a good idea to have a book or a magazine with you. That way, if they're late, you can read. Or you can just try to get to the next level of Candy Crush Saga on your phone. You could even hide your phone **INSIDE** a book so you look all deep and mysterious.

Date: "Sorry I'm a bit late..."

You: "That's okay—just catching up on a little light reading."

Date: "Wow, *The Big Book of Contemporary American Poetry.* SWOON. You are so deep and interesting...."

3. Have an idea where to go.

Ideally you will have already covered what you're going to do on your date when you did the asking out, but if not, have at least a couple of suggestions up your sleeve.

Kiss?

You don't want this to happen:

You: "what do you want to do?"

Your date: "I dunno, what do you want to do?"

You: "whatever."

Your date: "I don't mind, whatever you feel like."

You: "I'm easy. It's up to you."

Your date: "whatever. You pick."

You: "Nah, you."

Hey! How did you know what happens when I go out on a date?

I mean, please. Something like this might be a little better:

You: "what do you want to do?"

Your date: "I don't know, what do you want to do?"

You: "well, we could check out the new Marvel movie or go for a walk in the park or just wander around the mall."

Your date: "The movie sounds great."

You: "Wonderful."

Your date: "Lovely."*

*If you really talk like this you are: (a) straight out of a cheesy romance novel, (b) in need of more help than this little book can offer, or (c) Prince William.

In my case, I'm going to go for *b*.

One way of tackling the whole "what to do?" thing is to let your date choose.

If they leave it up to you, then pick something you will both enjoy.

First dates that take place at the nearest skate park are usually also last dates. Unless, of course, your date is also really into skateboarding.

Movies are a pretty safe bet. There is probably something playing that you would both like to see, and it will also mean you can be together without having to talk the whole time:

- **No embarrassing pauses in conversation.**
- **No trying to think of what to say next.**
- **And you'll have something to talk about afterward.**

But remember, just because you want to see *REVENGE OF THE NUNS IN CHAIN-SAW HELL IV*...

A classic movie—but not as good as *Mutant Toxic Bikini Girls Go Splat.*

...doesn't mean your date will want to. Have a conversation and find something that you're **BOTH** going to enjoy.

4. Talk.

Blah, blah, blah, blah, blah, blah, blah, blah, blah, blah, blah, blah, blah.

Whatever you end up doing with your date, you are going to have to talk to the other person at some point.

It can't be helped—that's what dates are all about.

It can be a little daunting; it can seem embarrassing; you might think you sound stupid. And nerves can get the better of you.

You might want to say:
"That was a good movie, wasn't it?"

But what comes out is:
"Wibble, yipple, pipple, pong, belch."

Just relax. Here's a secret: **CRUSHES ARE PEOPLE, TOO.** They will forgive you if you get your words backward or if you make a bad joke. They are as nervous as you are.

But if you are worried about those **L O N G**, embarrassing pauses, just remember to follow a few simple rules:

- *Listen to your date.* There is no point thinking up something witty to say if you haven't been paying any attention to what they've been saying.

• **Don't be a bore.** Your date isn't with you to be lectured to about why Cam Newton is a football god, how Twenty Øne Piløts rocks, or why Kendall Jenner is every guy's dream girl.

Blah, blah, blah, blah, blah, blah, blah, blah...Hello? Hello?

ZZZZZZZZZZZ.

• **Don't go on and on and on and on and on and on about yourself, either.** The whole point of a good conversation is that it goes two ways. It's fine to drop in little things about yourself, but don't sit down and tell your date your life story—unless, of course, they ask.

I was born on a dark and stormy night....

• **Ask questions.** Most people like, and are good at, talking about themselves. Asking questions will show that you are interested in this person and want to find out more. It's also a good idea to ask questions that don't require just a yes-or-no answer. That means "Which part of the movie did you like best?" is better than "That was a good movie, wasn't it?"

• **Share some little secrets.** The fastest way to get

to know someone better is to tell them something about you that is personal and not obvious. On the other hand, you don't want to scare them away by getting too intimate too quickly. DO NOT overshare. It's a date—not therapy—and it's meant to be fun. So recounting the hot dream you had last night is probably NOT a good idea.

> Can I smell your hair? Hello? Date? Why are you running away?

- **Don't rush to fill every breath with a joke or a story.** *Every conversation has some silences.*
- **Relax.** *Be yourself. The whole point of a date is that you are trying someone on for size—seeing if they fit, seeing if you hit it off, seeing if you like each other enough to go on another date. And MAYBE another and another.*

> Oh, sure. That's easy for you to say.

5. Think about the money question beforehand.

This is a tough one.

> Cash, dinero, dough, moola.

If you want to pay for your date, that's fine—that's your privilege, but no one should expect it to be their right.

If you are going to the movies, you might want to offer to

pay—most people will then buy the popcorn or pick up a pizza afterward.

But if you decide to be Little Mr. Flashy Pants and take your date somewhere expensive, make sure you've got the dollars to cover it, because it isn't fair to expect your date to chip in.

Whatever you do, don't, don't, don't tell someone you would like to take them out and then turn up broke and have to resort to a hot date sitting in a bus shelter. If you've got no money, then let them know subtly when you ask them out or make a plan that doesn't require spending anything. Suggest a walk in the park and an ice cream—cheap, cool, and pretty romantic. Remember: You don't have to have great wads of cash to go on a good date.

6. Don't forget you're on a date.

If you run into some friends, don't go off with them and ignore your date. And if you do see someone you know, don't try to hide the fact that you're on a date, either.

If you act like you're embarrassed to be with your date, it will probably be your last one. But also don't parade them around. Your date isn't a trophy or a new pair of sneakers for your friends to admire and make comments about.

Do any of these things and you will, to be frank, look like a jerk. And your date will hate it.

While we're on the subject of things that your date might hate...let's talk about PHONES. It might be fun to Instagram your walk in the park, you might both get a kick out of taking a selfie together, and there is no reason why you or your date shouldn't check in to WhatsApp. But spending the entire time on your phone will kinda get in the way of your plans, and your date might not be quite as glued to their phone as you are. They might think it's a little rude. Here's a crazy idea...once your date has started, why not put the phone away and get to know the person you're with? You don't need a Wi-Fi connection to do that.

> So I can't live stream my date to my millions of followers? Well, hundreds. Well, my mom. All right, all right...TO MY CAT.

7. Offer to walk your date home.

It's only polite and shows that you care that your date gets home safely. But if they say they'll be okay, don't make a big deal about how dangerous the streets are and how you're the big man and you must protect them. You're not Superman. The days of knights in shining armor are long gone. It's the twenty-first century, not the twelfth. It's nice to show you care about someone being safe—it's the right thing to do—but don't make it into some sort of macho BS. Instead, just ask your date to text you when they get home safe. Not only does it show that you care about them, but it also paves the way for you to ask them out for *another* date. Although maybe not that night—that could seem a bit **NEEDY.**

So everything has gone well. You've had a great date. They've:

- *laughed at your jokes,*
- *listened to your stories,*
- *enjoyed the movie,*
- *and shared a milk shake with you at McDonald's.*

You are a success. The date is a success. But now comes the trickiest problem of all...

The Kiss Good Night

It's about time!

Wow—that's always a real toughie....

When?

Where?

How?

Tongue or no tongue?

But what if my breath smells, our teeth clank, or our noses get all smooshed?

Don't panic: The kiss good night can be really nice and not as nerve-racking as you might think.

The difficult thing is that someone has to make the first move; otherwise you'll never get around to touching lips or tickling tongues.

So this is the scene:

The night's been great, and you've walked your date to their bus stop or house.

And then you stop.

You say thanks for coming.

Your date says thanks for a great time.

You both stand and do a swirly, twisty little dance on the spot.

You both look at each other.

You both giggle a little and then...

NOTHING. Hey—I've been there before.

But that's where a kiss should come in.

So what do you do?

Well, while you're giggling and twirling, you could reach out your hand. Your date might understand what you're trying to do, and take it.

Zowee!

Wow—you've touched. Pretty electric stuff.

Now, just let your hand, still holding theirs, fall to your side. Unless you've both got incredibly **S t r E T c H y** arms, you're going to have to move closer together.

We are not talking about pulling your date to you like a fish on the end of a line—just letting your hand and arm suggest a movement that gets your date closer to you.

How close?

About the length of your nose. That's close.

Now is the time for courage.

The time for the **Kiss.**

Reach in gently and plant a delicate kiss on your date's lips or, if you want to take it more slowly, their cheek. You'll then know for dead certain whether they want you to kiss them again, because if they do, they'll kiss you back.

It's all very simple. The key is reading the signals—those little signs that let you know when the time is right and whether your date wants to be kissed at all.

All the
giggling,
looking into each other's eyes,
holding hands,
gently touching each other's arms or back.

Little things like these. And when you get to the moment of truth, you'll find:
your faces very close together,
yourselves looking into each other's eyes,
the conversation has dried up,
you're both glancing at each other's mouth,
yourselves kissing.

Wow
　Yippee
　　Home run
　　　Houston, we have touched down!

And the really great thing about the **Kiss Good Night**? It can actually happen at almost any point during your date. It doesn't HAVE to be at the end—the "good night" bit is just the most traditional point to pucker up and get your smooch on. So keep those lips at DEFCON 1 and ready to go, because you never know when a kiss might happen!

Now we come to that eternal question: **To tongue or not to tongue?**

Sometimes people like to kiss with their mouths open and use their tongues to explore. As gross as that sounds, it actually feels very nice, although it might take a little bit of getting used to. It's called French-kissing—although it has nothing to do with the French. If you don't want to French-kiss, or your date doesn't want to, then there is no rule that says you have to.

Je t'aime, oui, oui, oh là là—wanna kiss?

Kissing isn't a simple matter of *A, B, C.*

Sometimes a quick **LIP-LOCK** is wonderful; sometimes an end-of-the-world **Tasty Tongue Kiss** is the only thing that will do. But for your first kiss, it's probably best to err on the side of caution.

Remember these basic kissing rules, which apply just as well for the first kiss good night as for any other time you kiss someone:

- ***Don't*** *lunge at your date as if you're trying to tackle them.*
- ***Don't*** *try to force your tongue down the other*

person's throat. You're kissing, not trying to find out what they had for lunch.

Gross!

- **Don't** *assume that just because you've been out on a date, you have the right to a kiss. You don't. And your date doesn't have the right to kiss you or to expect a kiss from you, either.*
- **Don't** *assume that just because you've had a quick kiss, things are automatically going to go further.*

- **Do** *pick your place—somewhere that isn't too busy and where neither of your parents will suddenly make an appearance.*
- **Do** *make sure, if it's outside your date's house, that the parents can't see. Your date might feel uncomfortable about having a quick kiss with Mom watching through the window.*
- **Do** *take your time.*
- **Do** *enjoy it.*

However, if there isn't any giggling, your date is walking quickly ahead of you with her arms crossed, and the conversation is of the one-word "Yes" or "No" variety, then there probably isn't going to be a kiss. Don't take it personally—sometimes dates just don't work out. If that's the case, it's time to bow

out and admit that it wasn't meant to be.
No hard feelings.

It's possible
that your date
just doesn't feel ready to kiss you yet. If you've obviously gotten along well, then they'd probably still like to go on another
date. Remember to read those signs. Each situation is different.

Dates can be a nightmare, but they don't have to be. From
asking someone out to kissing them good night, the key to the
whole thing is to take your time, be yourself, and never, ever forget that you are with another person—not a cardboard cutout
but a real person who has **interests**, *feelings*, and EMOTIONS
just like you.

If it doesn't work out—don't worry about it. It happens.
Sometimes two people who should get along just can't stand
each other after they've spent some time together one-on-one.
Just move on.

Always remember that both people in every great romantic
duo and in every old married couple, as well as movie stars,
rock gods, and supermodels, have all had first dates.

Relax—enjoy them.

An Exception to the Rule

All of the above information is really useful, funny, informa-
tive, and good value for the money. Good job for reading it...

you should probably read it again...and then once more just for luck. It is THAT good. High fives all around.

But—there is always a *but*...and this *but* is something that can catch even the most experienced dater by surprise.

It's **THE DATE THAT ISN'T A DATE** aka **THE ACCIDENTAL DATE.**

Because all the "asking out" and "making plans" and "getting ready" stuff isn't the only way to have a date.

You might have a friend...

You might really like each other...

They make you laugh...

You make them laugh...

You hang out together—a lot...

You go to the movies together...

To the mall...

To the skate park...

You are constantly texting each other...

Liking each other's Insta posts...

And generally spending a lot of time together.

And then, before you know it, you're hanging out on a Saturday afternoon at the mall, and you've supersized at Mickey-D's before sharing a jumbo popcorn (half sweet, half salt—because that's how *she* likes it) while watching Chris Pratt blow up the galaxy in IMAX.

And that, my friend, is **A DATE.** (And a pretty good one at that.)

No one asked anyone.

No plans were made.

No special outfits were chosen.

No aftershave was splashed in strategic places.

No one said anything about being on a date, going on a date, or wanting a date.

You might not even be alone—you might be surrounded by a group of your mutual friends. A group-hang with a ton of people.

You're just doing what you do, with your friend, but suddenly **EVERYTHING IS DIFFERENT.**

There may even be a kiss.

Well, that isn't confusing at all, is it?

And just in case things aren't confusing enough, all that stuff about the **ACCIDENTAL DATE** just happening, as if by magic—the person you're with might still consider it to have been just two friends hanging. So it's best to err on the side of caution. You can always slip something like this into the conversation: "This is so weird, it kinda feels like A DATE," and watch how they react. If they smile and nod—you're probably on the same page. If they spend four minutes laughing and have to sit down for a glass of water—you might only be buds.

Dates are funny old things....You can plan them, think about them for hours, strategize about what to say and wear, and even accidentally find yourself right in the middle of one, but ultimately the best dates are the ones where you just relax and have fun.

You could have just said that at the beginning and saved us all a lot of time and effort!

THE NEXT STEPS

The date has gone great.

You had a kiss good night.

You are totally psyched because...

Your crush LikEs YOU.

Excellent. Congratulations.

Thank you very much! It was nothing, really.

Now what?

Well, going into school the next day and telling all your friends that you made out with so-and-so from History class is a big no-no.

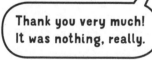

But all my friends ask me for details!

As is splashing it all over social media.

Why?

Well, just think about it for a minute.

It's natural to feel great if you hit it off with someone—you feel happy and even proud.

It's natural to want to tell as many people as possible so they'll all know how happy you are and maybe even so you can brag about it a little bit.

But remember that you are talking about **SOMEONE ELSE**—someone you supposedly like.

The other person might not want the

    whole school,

        basketball team,

            Twitterverse,

                and entire world

to know that you had a quick kiss in the park and that you tried to put your hand up her shirt.

If you make out with someone, it's always best to assume that they want to keep it a secret. At least for a little while. When you first start seeing someone, when you first become a couple, it takes a little while for you both to get used to the idea.

It takes a while for you to stop going,

"Wow. We are actually going out. I can't believe it."

And oddly enough, that's why when we first start dating someone, we want to tell other people—because it makes it all seem more real to us.

CONFUSED?

HERE'S HOW IT GOES:

1. You go out on a date with Little Miss (or Mr.) Gorgeous.
2. You and LMG make out with each other.
3. You and LMG decide to become an "item."
4. You can't believe that you and LMG are going out.
5. You tell all your friends about going out with LMG because that makes it more real. If your friends know, it must be true.
6. LMG dumps you because they didn't want anyone to know right away.

BUMMER.

If you really are bursting to tell someone, then just tell one friend who you can trust not to spread the news around. Better still, write it down in a journal or a letter to yourself.

Dear Me,

I'm going out with someone gorgeous. I can't believe it—but now that I've written it down, it must be true. Wow.

Sincerely,

Me

Once you've both gotten used to the idea that you're a couple, then it might be nice to let people know. You don't have to set up a joint Instagram account or anything. Just hold hands in public, be seen together, snuggle together.

People will get the idea.

However, if you are dating someone and after a few weeks, or even a few months, they still don't want people to know you're together, then it might be a good idea to ask why.

Just as it's not natural to rush out and put up posters announcing that you're an item, it's also not natural *never* to tell anyone.

It might mean that they aren't happy about something, or they feel a little embarrassed, or they might just be very shy. Not everyone likes to live their private life in public.

BuZZ, CRACKLE...This is WKSS with an important news flash. I have a new babe. I repeat, I have a new girlfriend.

If you want to go public and he or she doesn't, sit and talk about it. There is probably a very good reason. Remember, talking is the best thing you can ever do. Well, maybe not the best thing—but we'll talk about that later.

Nudge, nudge, wink, wink, say no more.

MAKING A RELATIONSHIP WORK

(Batteries not included.)

(Also known as BEING ROMANTIC.)

Just because you've gone out with someone a few times doesn't mean you can sit back on your heels and relax. The toughest challenge is yet to come.

You've got to make your relationship work.

How do you do that?

Well, with something that guys of all ages find difficult, embarrassing, and sometimes downright impossible. It's called *romance*.

Is that flowers and stuff?

Romance is very important, because when the romance goes, your whole relationship begins to fizzle.

IT'S TRUE.

You can lust after someone, love them so much you feel like you're floating, but the day the romance dies is the day the clock starts counting down to the big split between the two of you.

So how do you capture the romance of a relationship and keep it? Well, when you first meet someone, everything that person says and does is romantic. **THEY CAN BURP, FART, OR THROW UP, AND YOU'LL THINK IT'S CUTE, ENDEARING, AND SWEET.**

But once you've been with someone a little bit longer, that's when the romance can begin to disappear—when you know exactly what your sweetheart is about to say, do, or even think.

And that's when you've got to roll up your sleeves and start working at romance, because if you don't nurture your relationship it will stick its little legs in the air, roll over, and kick the bucket.

What Is Romance?

Anything.
Everything.

All the expected stuff—flowers, **chocolates,** cute little texts full of hearts and smiley faces, **love letters.** That's all romantic.

But remember, if you are being romantic, keep it simple. A single flower can be just as romantic as a huge bunch of roses and a massive box of chocolates. In fact, if you go too far overboard, it can become embarrassing, and instead of being flattered or touched, your girlfriend or boyfriend will feel awkward and uncomfortable.

The key to real romance is to use your head. That's why a bologna sandwich and a can of soda at the right time, in the right place, with the right person, can be so much more romantic than a four-course meal in a fancy restaurant.

Romance is at its best when it's simple and when some thought has been put into it. Anyone, if they've got the cash, can take a girl to the movies, buy her chocolates, and then whisk her off to dinner. That's not true romance—that's just easy.

True romance is all about creating or buying something special to give to someone you love that only the two of you will understand. It's about demonstrating that you "get them" in a way that other people don't. That's why a plastic frog—if your loved one is crazy about **PLASTIC FROGS**—can be just as romantic as a diamond ring.

And a lot cheaper, too!

What else is romantic?

Well, it doesn't have to involve the giving of gifts. Just taking time to be with someone can be romantic. It's very easy when you've been with someone for a while to take them for granted—to forget just how special they are and how lucky you are to be with them. Telling someone how much you love them is the most romantic thing. But:

- *walking in the park,*
- *sitting on a beach in the middle of winter,*
- *telling stories,*
- *sharing jokes and secrets,*
- *and just cuddling up and burying your face in their hair for hours*

can also be very romantic.

BUT BE CAREFUL.

Some guys get it all wrong and are romantic *all the time*. Do that and you'll probably end up being shown the door.

No one can stand being given gifts, sent letters, or being lovey-dovey every moment of the day.

It would drive you crazy.

Romance should be thought about, rationed, made special—it's not for every day.

And giving someone a bunch of flowers or walking in the park won't save your relationship if it's already over. No matter how romantic you are, if you and your girlfriend are destined to walk away from each other, you're going to, no matter what. Romance won't save a relationship, but it can help to stop it from going downhill to begin with.

> No chance of a touchdown in overtime?

Romance should be fun, exciting, tingly, and wonderful. It's all about losing yourself in someone else. It's probably the best thing there is in the entire world, and you can't be in love without it. And we guys really can do it. There aren't any big secrets to being romantic—just use your imagination and keep it simple.

LOVE

What Is Love, Anyway?

That is not a simple question to answer. Love is not something that can be put into words.

Poets, writers, and singers have spent hundreds of years trying to say what it is that makes love *love*, what it is that makes us feel so very much for one particular person, what it is that makes us want to **laugh, sing, and dance** every time we see that person.

> Hey, that's how I feel when my football team wins.

Only one thing is for sure: Love is not easy. It's not straightforward, and there are absolutely no rules about falling in love with someone.

You can meet someone and after a couple of hours you love them completely, or you can be friends with a person for years and years and then suddenly wake up one day and discover that you've fallen head over heels in love with them.

However, there *are* certain things that love *isn't* about:

- ***It isn't about controlling someone or getting them to do something they don't want to do.***
- ***It isn't about saying "I love you" just to get someone to make out with you.***
- ***It isn't about trying to change someone to make them into the kind of person YOU want them to be.***

How Do You Know It's Love?

Who can tell?

Sometimes you are with someone and you just know.

You look at them and you just know that this is a person you don't want to be without.

One way of being sure that you really do love someone is to sit yourself down and ask yourself some questions before you tell them.

Me: "Do I love this person?"

Me 2: "Yes. I think so."

Me: "Are you sure, Me 2?"

Me 2: "Well, I think I'm sure."

Me: "Do you think about them a lot?"

Me 2: "All the time. I can't think of anything else."

Me: "Do you long to be with them?"

Me 2: "Oh, yes. They're great. They make me feel kind of whole and special."

Me: "Would you feel absolutely devastated if you could never see them again?"

Me 2: "Do sour—cream— and—onion potato chips make your breath smell like the inside of an old jockstrap?"

I wouldn't know— I never eat old jockstraps.

Me: "Do you like them more than Jennifer Lawrence?"

Me 2: "Jennifer who?"

Me: "Maybe you've just got a crush?"

Me 2: "Maybe. But I really think it's more than that. I'm in LOVE."

Me: "You sure you're sure?"

Me 2: "Yes. Yes, I am."

If you're being honest with yourself, you probably know in your heart of hearts whether you are really in love with someone or just have a crush on them, because one thing that love does demand is mountains of honesty.

When you are in love with someone, you have to be honest with yourself and with that person. It's tough—but that's the deal.

Sometimes it's nice to think you're in love, or to con yourself into thinking that you're in love, because there is nothing nicer than feeling that safe and wanted.

But be careful not to confuse LOVE and LUST.

Even though they are both exciting feelings, they *are* different. Lust tends to be purely sexual interest, while love involves deeper feelings. One good rule for telling the difference is this: If you like talking to your squeeze as much as you like kissing them, you might be falling in love. But if you really just like the kissing part, it might be only lust you're feeling.

What About Crushes?

What's the difference between being in love and having a crush? And how can we not mistake one for the other?

Well, a crush is like falling in love with someone that you might never get together with or someone you don't know at all. It might be your teacher, a rock star, a supermodel, or just someone in your school.

Crushes are usually fairly intense, and the person you've got the crush on is all you can think about for a while.

But it isn't love. Or at least it isn't...yet. If you are lucky, a crush CAN turn into something more, but it's best not to expect it to.

Crushes are based more on fantasy than anything else. It's the *idea* of that person that is so exciting.

In fact, if you and the object of your crush ever did get together, you might be hugely disappointed.

Crushes are also a big part of the way that you get to understand your own particular sexuality.

When you hit puberty, it's not just your body that changes—your mind and feelings undergo a pretty major upheaval, too.

You become aware of your own sexuality and you start feeling attracted to certain people.

It's all normal, and it's all natural.

After a while things move on and you find a different person to have a crush on.

You never really grow out of crushes, but they get a little less intense and a little more fun as you get older.

Saying "I Love You"

So you've just fallen **HEAD OVER HEELS,** out-of-control, end-of-the-world in love with someone.

That's great.

But now you want to tell them.

That isn't so great.

Admitting that someone matters that much to you can be particularly tough for us guys.

But it's important.

Why?

Because it's the way relationships grow—and besides, this person may just feel the same way about you. Imagine you are with the person you love. You can't help it. You're about to burst, so you tell them. And they say it back! Now, not only are you in love, but you're in love *together*.

Of course, there are all the worries and fears that when you finally get up the nerve to say "I love you," she or he is going to:

laugh,

Yup.

slap you,

Oh, yeah.

or go, "what did you say?"

Very probably.

But very few people will do any of the above.

When you tell someone that you love them, it's obvious that you are laying yourself on the line. You are being very honest and open about your feelings, and only the most heartless person in the world would laugh at you after you've revealed something so personal.

So the best thing to do is **TRUST YOUR JUDGMENT** and pick the right time to let this person know just how you feel.

Like gym class?

So don't say it:

over the phone,

in a letter, in a text, or via Snapchat,

just as you are saying good night,

after an argument,

surrounded by friends,

or in a movie theater.

Go somewhere that's private, but don't build the whole thing up and don't, don't, don't go down on one knee.

You're not proposing.

You got that right!

Just take a deep breath and come out with it. Just say,

"I love you."

Simple.

Now what? Well, don't expect to hear "I love you" back. That isn't why you said it, and besides, having someone tell you that he has fallen in love with you can be something of a shock—they'll probably need a little time to get used to the idea and think about what you've just said.

You hope they feel the same way, but unfortunately it doesn't always work out like that. It's a risk you have to take. Just think—if you never said it, you might never know their true feelings.

Uh-oh.

So what can you do if the girl (or guy) of your dreams, who you have just declared your undying love to, turns around and says: "That's very sweet, but I don't love you."

Not much, I'm afraid.

You've just got to get up, dust yourself off, and accept it. There's no point getting angry, bitter, or aggressive. There is no point trying to win them over with love letters, flowers, or gifts. There is no point trying to force someone to love you.

It doesn't work that way.

The only thing you can do is accept it and feel sad.

And go back to watching TV!

Falling in love is the best thing that can happen to you.

> Surely not as good as winning the Super Bowl?

And it will happen.

There really is someone for everyone, and just about everybody finds someone to fall in love with and be loved by.

> Is that a promise?

So don't worry—just keep on looking.

GETTING INTIMATE

> Making out! Getting it on! Doing the wild thing!

You've gotten past the first date.

You've gotten past becoming an item. You might've even fallen in love.

Getting intimate is just another dilemma to face.

It's natural: You're with someone who you think is pretty neat, and they think you are pretty neat, so you want to explore and touch and cuddle.

But it's important that you get intimate with someone for all the right reasons and not all the wrong ones.

So what are these WRONG reasons?

Wrong Reasons

Don't go there!

1. All your friends claim to have done it.

They haven't—guys are terrible braggers. When we get together, we love to make up stories. We shouldn't, but we do. Almost every guy brags about his conquests, and almost every guy is making it up. And besides, even if your best friend has *actually* undone a girl's bra, that doesn't mean you have to do the same. Take your time.

2. You took someone to a movie or bought them a pizza.

So you took someone out—it doesn't mean they owe you. That's just ridiculous. If you think that, you really need to do some serious reconsidering. When someone gives you a hug, it's because they want to, not because you bought them a present.

3. You've said "I love you."

Intimacy and love are two different things. It's nice when they happen together—but they don't always, so if you get one, don't automatically expect the other.

4. You've been dating for a given length of time.

You can be with someone for years before you both feel ready to commit to any kind of physical love. Everyone gets to make his or her own rules about becoming intimate. It's much better to wait until you, and your partner, feel the time and the person are right.

5. Your friends say your sweetheart has done it before with another guy.

I mean...really? You are **REALLY** going to fall for that one? For one thing, IF IT IS EVEN TRUE, so what? Just because someone might have had sex before doesn't automatically mean that they are "open for business" with you. Even if they have, it's none of your friends' business, and unless your bae chooses to talk to you about it, it's none of YOUR business. And if it matters that much to you, then you probably need to get on the bus, make your way down to Big Al's World of Mirrors, find the biggest display you can, and take a good, hard, long look at yourself. Gossip is a horrible, nasty, vicious thing. Ignore what the **HATERS** and **TROLLS** are saying, and listen to the only two people who are important—your squeeze and your conscience. Everybody has a past. Some people have MORE of a past than others. It's a fact of life.

Haters keep on hating!

6. You've seen it on the Internet and want to give it a try.

Dude...? Just because you watched clips of Alexander Rossi winning the Indy 500 on YouTube, it doesn't mean you'd walk up to him and ask to take his car out for a spin. Same deal here…but more on the whole **PORN** thing later.

I'd rather watch cats doing funny things on YouTube.

And remember, NO always means NO—it doesn't mean *maybe*, *persuade me*, or *yes*. If you're with someone and you're having a snuggle on the sofa and they want to stop, YOU'VE GOT TO STOP.

And if someone you're attracted to is passed out at a party, or drunk and out of it, it is NOT OKAY to try to get intimate with them. These are not, and never will be, excuses:

- *Well, they haven't ACTUALLY said NO, so what I'm doing is okay.*
- *They haven't ACTUALLY pushed my hand away, so they must not mind.*
- *They haven't ACTUALLY stopped me from taking pictures on my phone, so it's okay to put them all over Facebook.*
- *No one has ACTUALLY stopped the other guys and I don't want to look like I'm a coward, so I better join in.*

Because here's a news flash—not only is it **TOTALLY NOT OKAY**, it's also illegal and you could find yourself in a lot of trouble with the LAW.

It's also a real **DOUCHE** thing to do.

Basically, if someone is too drunk or out of it to say YES—you've got to assume it's a NO, even if they don't say it. It's called **CONSENT** and if someone doesn't give it, you can't take it.

And likewise, if you want to stop, IT'S GOT TO STOP.

There is huge pressure on guys to somehow prove they are real men by hooking up with as many people as possible. But you really don't have to if you don't want to. Rather than proving your manhood, this kind of "love 'em and leave 'em" attitude only does one thing: It sends up a giant red flag for everyone else to stay away from you.

What About the Right Reasons?

Well, there really is only one right reason: because you want to share something special and be close to someone who means a lot to you.

If you or your significant other is thinking about making some sort of physical commitment, the most important thing is not sweet music, low lights, or a romantic setting. The most important thing is to talk, so that you both know what you want.

Getting intimate is great.

It's wonderful, end-of-the-world, lose-yourself-in-someone great.

But if it's not with the right person, or if you find yourself going further than you want to and feeling uncomfortable, it can also be lousy. The lousiest thing in the world. So take your time, decide what's right for you, and make sure your partner knows how you feel and you know how they feel.

Get that right, and a hug will make time stand still.

For what it's worth, remember it is illegal to have sex if you are under a certain age. The age limit varies from state to state, falling anywhere between fourteen and eighteen years old. There are plenty of places online where you can find out what it might be for your state, and it can be different ages for gay and straight sex—so do your homework. No, a policeman probably won't break down your bedroom door and arrest you on the spot, but these laws exist for a reason—to protect you.

And remember, if you should find yourself with someone under a pile of coats at a party or down in the rec room on a rainy Wednesday afternoon and something happens—all the responsibilities are still there.

It doesn't make a difference if you've known someone nine months or nine hours....Treat them with some R.E.S.P.E.C.T.

(Here's a crazy idea—why not get yourself a condom, stash it under your Dairy Queen loyalty card in the back of your wallet, and forget about it? At least it will be there if all of a sudden you find yourself in the **MOMENT OF NEED.**)

I could NEVER do that. It would be way too embarrassing to have THAT in my wallet. I'm Burger King all the way.

Which brings us nicely to...

Safe Sex

If you and your bae have decided you're ready to become intimate, then you should be mature and responsible enough to go about it *safely*. Yes, sex can be wonderful, but there are a lot of things that can go wrong, too.

First of all, as you learned in Biology class, the functional reason for sex is to reproduce—in other words, to make babies. Now, if you aren't ready to have a rug rat running around your room while you're doing your homework, be sure that you and your girlfriend take the appropriate precautions—before the fact.

The most common method of pregnancy prevention is to use a condom. Condoms are also crucial in preventing the spread of disease—everything from common sexually transmitted diseases (STDs) like herpes, gonorrhea, chlamydia, and syphilis, which have unpleasant and pretty serious symptoms, to HIV/AIDS. HIV/AIDS is increasingly manageable thanks to improvements in medicines, and people can now live with the disease for their entire lives, but it is still really nasty and can be deadly.

A condom is your "go to" whenever it comes to sex, whether it's with a girl or with a guy. It's sort of like a one-fingered glove that fits over your penis and catches the semen so it never enters your partner's body. You should be aware, however, that **CONDOMS AREN'T FOOLPROOF**—they *can* break.

Most drugstores sell them, and any package of condoms has detailed instructions about how to put one on. It might not be a bad idea to practice at home, to be sure you know what you're doing before you really *need* to know. And another thing: You're the one who wears it, so you should be the one who has it on hand. Don't expect the other person to take care of it for you.

Better to be prepared and not need it than to need it and not be prepared.

Or is it...be prepared and need it?

Or maybe it's...not be prepared and not need it?

Or is it...be not needed and be not unprepared?

Or something...whatever...
JUST CARRY A CONDOM.

I'm always prepared!

Now, you may think, "I know my partner. They don't have any kind of disease." But what you need to realize is that when you have sex with them, you're also having sex with anyone else they have ever had sex with—at least from a disease standpoint.

Oh...gross...

And since you have no idea what those people are like, or who they in turn may have had sex with, you can never be too careful.

When you come right down to it, the only no-risk, truly reliable way to avoid pregnancy and disease is not to have sex. But if you feel you're ready, be mature enough to be responsible— to yourself and to your partner.

If you need more information on safe sex, take a look at the resources section at the end of this book.

Sex and the Internet

There is another way to become intimate with someone, and it can be no less intense and carry no less responsibility than the more "traditional" way.

And that is through the awesome power of **TECHNOLOGY.** Your phone, your laptop, your tablet—they can all connect you with millions of other people, and that is great. But with the AWESOME POWER of TECHNOLOGY also comes some pretty

AWESOME RESPONSIBILITY. (I think Spider-Man's uncle said something like that—cool guy, knows a thing or two.)

You may start texting, emailing, or messaging someone—it might be someone you met playing *Call of Duty: Black Ops 2* online, it might be someone from school, or it might be someone you barely know. And before you know it, you start thinking you have feelings for this person.

It's kinda crazy: You've never met them, or you've hardly spent any time with them. You might not even know what they look like—but there is something there. You message **A LOT**. It feels really good to be able to share with someone, to be totally honest and have them **GET YOU.** They listen. You feel you can be yourself more easily. You get a little flutter of excitement when you see a new message in your in-box.

Soon your messages might move on from just chatting about stuff to an altogether "spicier" style of conversation. Something more personal and intimate. Talking about how you'd like to be with them: hugging and kissing...and...(you know what I'm talking about...).

I'm not sure that I do. I'm pure as the snow. Honest.

You might even be tempted to send someone a selfie—but one that has less to do with your face and more to do with another part of your body.

You're not talking about my elbow, are you?

Some people call sending racy messages and sexy pics **SEXTING.**

Just because lots of other guys do it, does that mean it's okay?

Ummmm... yes?

Well, it isn't without its problems. You might think you're in love with someone you know only through the Internet. Or that you truly know them and trust them. But is that really the case? It's easy to try to convince yourself that what you feel is real, but if you decide to get intimate via a screen, there are just as many, if not more, things that you need to think about.

You might think, "What's the harm? It's just a few pictures, it's just fun. It doesn't hurt anyone."

Well...**DING DING DING DING**...wake up and smell the coffee, bro, because it **AIN'T ALWAYS LIKE THAT.**

So it's more like a decaf soy latte?

Here are a few things you might want to consider before sharing your **JUNK** digitally:

- Does the person receiving your messages and pictures even want them? They might not. And if they don't, it's called sexual harassment, which is a type of bullying. And that could get you in a lot of trouble. Trouble with the law, with your school, with your parents. The full house.

- If the person sharing this hot-and-horny exchange is under the age of consent, you could find yourself in hot water with the law. The age of consent varies from state to state, so even if it's legal in your state, it might not be in the one the picture is coming from. And while we are talking about not being legal: If the person sending you a picture *is* under the age of consent, they could get in a whole heap of trouble, because the law would consider the messages distribution of child pornography. That is beyond bad news for everyone, especially considering...

- Once a picture is on the Internet, it is REALLY hard to get rid of. If someone sends you a picture, it's not cool to share it anywhere online. Or to message it to your buds because you think it's cool or funny or to prove what a massive stud you are. If personal pictures get splashed all over the Internet without the consent of the person who sent them, you could, again, find yourself in a lot of trouble with the law. Lives have been destroyed because a massive **turd** pretending to be a guy has shared a naked picture of his girlfriend online. And likewise—any of the pictures you send could end up all over the

Internet. And it might take years and years for you to get rid of them.

Oh, man— that is not so great.

- And finally, if you don't know the person you are **SEXTING** with, if it's someone you've met only online and never in person, you don't know if they're even who they say they are. They MIGHT say they're called Kacie Lou, a blond cheerleader from LA. But you don't know that—even if they send you a picture of themselves, it might not be them. It's called being catfished, and it happens a lot more often than you might think. After all, it's not hard to find pictures of blond cheerleaders on the Internet—is it?

I wouldn't know. Honest...

You could actually be sharing all your intimate thoughts and pictures with a middle-aged guy called DWAYNE who thinks it's funny to pretend to be a cute cheerleader. And...you *really* don't want that.

So yeah, SEXTING sounds great, doesn't it? Getting in trouble with the police, destroying lives, guys called Dwayne...

I think that's called SARCASM.

One last thing about getting intimate via a screen. If you are lucky enough to have a special someone, a steady date, it does not automatically mean you should expect, demand, beg, or bully them into sending you a picture in their underwear. Even if you have sent them one of yourself in your boxers, even if you have told them you love them, even if you say you're going to delete it and never share it.

In fact, 51 percent of teenage girls say they have had pressure from a guy to send sexy messages or images. Sadly, that means 51 percent of teenage boys are dicks. Don't be one of the 51 percent—you are better than that.

Don't be one of the 51%!
Don't be one of the 51%!

BREAKING UP

Let's start with...

Dumping Someone

You might have thought it was tough getting up the nerve to ask your crush out, making your relationship public, and saying I love you. But none of that is as tough as saying it's all over.

No one enjoys dumping another person.

No one likes to see someone upset and sad.

No one likes that look on someone's face when you're about to tell them it's all over and they know what's coming but everything in their eyes is begging you not to say it.

That's a horrible moment.

But sometimes it's the only thing to do.

You can be with someone and love them a lot. They can make you laugh and be your best friend—but if it's time to move on, then it's time to say:

"I'M SORRY—IT'S ALL OVER."

Sometimes things just don't work out:

- *It's nobody's fault.*
- *It's not something that can be avoided.*
- *It just happens.*

A wise man once said that we might not be able to tell the moment when love begins, but we always know the exact moment it ends.

And that is so true.

You can't help falling in love, and you can't help falling out of love. But when you do want to break up, it's best to be honest, face up to your emotions, and respect your soon-to-be ex enough to let them know how you feel.

So the question is: Is there a right or wrong way to split up with someone?

No, not really. But there are some basic things that work when you dump someone, and some things that don't.

Golden Rule of Dumping Someone: Be honest and be strong.

Like The Rock?

Telling someone you've been close to that it's all over is never going to be easy. It's a rough ride, and it can be just as bad for the person doing the dumping as for the person being dumped. But no matter how much it hurts either of you, when you dump someone, you have to be **honest**. Decide what you want to do and do it. And that's when you have to be **STRONG**.

It's tough when you're faced with someone who is very upset, someone you care about. It's very tempting to say you're sorry and that you've changed your mind and that you'd like to try to work things out.

But the dumpee will hate your guts if you tell them it's all over and then let yourself be talked into trying to make it work out, only to realize after a while that you never wanted to give things a second chance to begin with.

Don't back down.

It's statistically proven that most couples who get to the

point of splitting up only to try to make things work out don't succeed. They end up going their separate ways, and there is even more heartache and pain when they finally do break up.

Remember: Decide what you want to do and do it.

Good advice.

Unfortunately, when you break up with someone, it's time for you to be a little selfish.

If YOU are unhappy in a relationship, YOU have to leave it.

If that means your soon-to-be ex is going to be upset, heartbroken, and cry, that's a real shame—and that should upset you as much as it upsets them. But ultimately it's true that no one wants to be with a guy if he isn't happy about being with them.

So by being true to your own feelings, you are doing the right thing, although the person being dumped might not see it that way at the time.

It isn't always going to be easy, and all too often you can find yourself wimping out and making some of the classic dumping mistakes.

Who are you calling a wimp?

So to help you avoid those mistakes, here are a few guidelines for dumping your girlfriend or boyfriend.

1. Where to Dump Someone

Just like for your first date, you have to pick the place carefully. Think about it. Striding up to the mall where your future ex is surrounded by all their friends and saying, **"SORRY, BABE—IT'S ALL OVER. I'M GOING OUT WITH YOUR BEST FRIEND,"** and then proceeding to make out with said best friend, is pretty mean. Pick a place where you know you can be alone and then break the news, so if they want to cry and get upset they can (and, equally important, so can you).

A good place is the other person's house, especially if you know that they're going to be there alone. You'll have somewhere that's private so there can be tears and talk, but it's also somewhere that you can leave when the time comes.

Things can get a little embarrassing if you dump someone at your house and then they refuse to leave until you take it all back.

Oh—I hadn't thought of that....

2. When to Dump Someone

Pick your moment carefully. You owe them that much.

Don't dump them just before they go on vacation, first thing in the morning at school, or just before exams start.

A good time is a Saturday afternoon—both of you will have the weekend to start getting over it, and friends should be available to lend support and a shoulder to cry on.

3. How to Dump Someone

You don't want to do the deed over the phone, by text, through social media, or in public. That's tacky and shows a lack of respect for the person you are splitting up with. You should always break up with someone face-to-face—and you never, ever, *ever* get a friend to dump someone for you.

Also, don't dump and run. If you're splitting up with someone, they have the right to be upset. Listen to what they have to say about splitting up and listen to how they feel about it. You have to face them and their tears.

And one of the biggest NO-NO'S is to take

the easy way out and start seeing someone else behind your current partner's back.

That's pretty cheap and nasty.

Why?

Because you're using that person to get you out of your current relationship. It shows that you just don't care enough to talk things through. If you do leave someone because you've met someone else, that's fine—it happens all the time. But it shows a huge lack of respect for yourself and the person you're dating if you don't finish one thing before you start another.

It's also not fair to make someone's life so miserable that they dump you. If you want to get out of the relationship, it's up to you to get out of it. Don't be nasty to them in front of your friends, don't stop phoning or texting, and don't pretend that they don't exist, in the hope that they'll get the message. That's the coward's way out.

And once you've dumped someone, don't, don't, don't make out with them the next time you're at a party together. Do, and there will be lots of anger and bitterness. And you'll have to go through the whole painful breakup process AGAIN.

4. What to Say

When you do finally tell someone it's all over, **BE TRUTHFUL** about why you want to split up—but don't be mean.

If there isn't a set reason, if you just feel that things aren't working out—say that. That's good enough in itself. Always remember that you're leaving someone because you want to, and never use the line "I'm doing this for your own good,"

because you're not, and it's very patronizing.

Don't:

- **Say anything hurtful:**

  "You're not good enough for me."

  "You were just a phase."

  "I only went out with you because I felt sorry for you."

- **Say anything condescending:**

  "You're too good for me."

  "I'll always love you."

  "It's not you—it's me."

- **Say anything untrue:**

  "I'll never love anyone else."

  "This hurts me more than it hurts you."

  "No, of course I'm not going out with your best friend."

DO:

- **Be clear and definite:**

  "This really is what I want. I'm sorry if that hurts you, but I think it's for the best."

- **Be kind:**

  "I've had a great time with you and I hope we can stay friends, although I understand you might not want that."

Getting Dumped

So that's how to dump someone. But what if **you** have been dumped?

Getting dumped hurts **MORE THAN ANYTHING ELSE IN THE WORLD.**

Having someone turn to you one day and say "I don't think we should see each other anymore" can make you feel like you've had the rug pulled out from under you, the sky is falling on your head, and you want to curl up into a ball and die.

You have every right to be upset, confused, and sad. But you don't have a right to make your ex's life miserable with phone calls at all hours, unexpected visits, or texts begging to get back together.

And although movies make it seem possible, it's not true that if you get dumped you can win someone back with flowers, poetry, or persistence. You can't. It's been decided. It's over. It's going to hurt.

One of the biggest challenges is not letting that sense of hurt and embarrassment turn into anger, not letting it persuade you that you'll feel better if you lash out: say mean things, spread gossip, trash the things they gave you, or "accidentally" post the sexy picture they sent you all over social media. As if somehow creating pain for the other person will cancel out the pain you feel. Because the reality is—it won't. All you'll do is lose respect.

The reality is that you're going to feel like there is nothing you can do to ever feel whole again. You're going to want to see your ex at every opportunity—and then hate them every time you do. Take the time to cry, to mourn the passing of love, to grieve—and then move on.

IT'S ONE OF THE TOUGHEST THINGS A GUY EVER HAS TO FACE, AND IT'S A TIME FOR COURAGE.

It isn't worth falling in love if you just end up getting hurt—is it?

And don't think that just because you're a guy you aren't allowed to get upset when someone dumps you. Don't think that you have to grin and bear it, take it on the chin, or shrug it off. You are allowed to cry, you are allowed to be upset, and you are allowed to feel like someone has ripped out your still-beating heart and jumped up and down on it. You feel sad—let it all out.

It's the best thing for you to do, really, because then you can try to start getting over the relationship. If you don't let out the tears and anger and hurt, then you may never be able to accept that it really is over.

There is no point trying to deny it, refusing to accept it, or trying to change it. Cry, watch action movies, listen to your favorite playlists, go for a run, talk to your mom, do whatever it takes to get rid of that gnawing emptiness that you feel inside—

but rest assured that it will go away. It might not feel like it at the time, but it will.

"Gnawing Emptiness"—isn't that a KISS song?

Getting Over It

Dumping and being dumped are the risks we all take when we fall in love, but if we didn't take those risks, we'd never find that special someone, and it's so worth it when you do.

Still, no one is ever ready to be **HEARTBROKEN,** and no one wants to be a **heaRtBReakeR.**

Fixing a broken heart isn't easy. There aren't any instant, just-add-water cures that allow a guy to control his feelings, heal his emotions, and get on with his life.

Hearts don't come with stick-on patches, they can't be fixed with spit and Scotch tape, and no matter how much we try to pretend that everything is fine, it usually isn't.

The only thing that will mend a broken heart is time.

Tick-tock, tick-tock.

If you've just been dumped— or if you've just dumped someone—it takes time to get over it. You might want to be by yourself a lot, to cry, and to feel blue. You might want to hang out with your friends and keep busy with sports. Whatever works for you...it's all fine and normal.

Some days you'll wake up and think that things are hopeless, that you'll never fall in love again, and that you'll be unhappy for the rest of your life.

But it does get better.

Slowly, and painfully, hearts heal.

Just don't expect it to happen overnight.

It's a rule of thumb that when someone dumps you, it can take at least as long to get over it as the length of time that you went out.

You won't be sad for that entire amount of time, and you won't mope around and be depressed. You'll probably date other people, maybe even have another long-term relationship. But to be totally, completely "I'm good with this, I really am" over someone can take a **_LONG, LONG TIME_**. Longer than most people realize.

And don't expect to stop loving someone just because you've been dumped. A broken heart isn't cured by trying to forget that you once really cared for someone, and it isn't about hating them.

When you really and truly fall in love with someone—no matter what happens—there will always be a part of you that will continue to care for them. That's normal and kind of nice, because it means that you'll never forget that person or the special time you had together.

This is important: You fell in love. It didn't work. You split up.

Don't try to substitute hate for love.

It's always better to remember the good times rather than the bad.

In fact, it will make you happier in the long term.

Really—it will.

And another thing: You don't mend a broken heart by jumping from one relationship to another. It's tempting. You feel low; you feel sad; you want a shoulder to cry on. A lot of guys do it. They split up with someone, or someone dumps them, and within days—maybe even hours—they're in another person's arms. Unfortunately, it rarely works out.

You can't substitute one emotion for another, and you can't substitute one person for another.

Except in sports.

You've got to give yourself time to get over one relationship before you move on to the next. If you don't give yourself enough time, you'll end up leapfrogging from one unhappy relationship to another, because it's a fact that if you start seeing someone when you're on the rebound, it doesn't last.

I'm on the rebound!

Getting over a serious relationship isn't an exact science. Different things work for different people—but no matter how you go about patching up your heart, dusting yourself off, and finding someone else to love, it's always best to give yourself time.

TIME IS A GREAT HEALER.

Now, before this book turns into a sappy romance, let's move on to the next chapter, which talks, among other things, about the old five-fingered shuffle...yep, masturbating.

CHAPTER TWO

SURVIVING ALL THE CHANGES IN YOUR BODY

THE PUBERTY EXPRESS

You hit puberty like an express train heading straight for Hormonesville, and all kinds of things begin to happen.

Both your body and mind change, and sometimes it's difficult to keep track of all the **WEiRD,** wacky, and *wonderful* things that are happening to you.

We'll deal with the mind stuff in the next chapter. This one is all about *bodies*.

Puberty for boys starts and stops anytime between ages ten and eighteen.

It's completely normal, and it doesn't make the slightest difference whether you're an early or late addition to the puberty club—the types of changes will be the same.

Let's kick off with the ol' **meat and two veg**.

Meat and two veg—that sounds like a good square meal. Oh...you don't mean...oh...

PLUMBING

Otherwise known as your **family jewels,** your **pride and joy,** your **PACKAGE,** your genitals.

Does your mom know you're saying this?

Boys have the bodily equivalent of the Bermuda Triangle covering the entire area of their genitals. And all through puberty, things seem to appear and disappear in this area for what seems like no reason at all, although hopefully no ships or planes will go missing inside your boxers.

So what actually happens?

For one thing, a boy's testicles and penis get bigger.

How big? Well, how long is a piece of string?

It varies, but not as much as you might think. Before puberty, a boy's penis is about one to two inches long when soft. After puberty, it's about two to four inches when soft and five to six inches when hard.

Now, before you all go running off to find a ruler, no two guys are the same.

Okay—but do you have a ruler I could borrow later?

And **sizE makEs no differEncE** as to how well it works.

If you're wondering whether the way you hang is the same as every other guy, it is, more or less. You'd be surprised just how similar all penises are. Sure, no two are the *same*, but they all follow the same *basic design*.

Does it have a trademark?

Yours might curve off to the side a little, or even curve up a little. **THAT'S PERFECTLY NORMAL**. Some guys have circumcised penises, which means that they have had an operation at some point in their lives to permanently pull back their foreskin, the piece of soft skin that covers the head of your penis. It doesn't affect the way it works or what it feels like to be the proud owner of one.

And some guys have only one testicle instead of the usual two. They're either born that way or have had one removed for medical reasons. If you have only one ball, it doesn't affect how it works, what it feels like, or whether you will be able to become a dad.

I wonder if anyone has ever had three?

So most penis-and-testicle sets are more or less the same, and they all do the same things. And when you hit puberty, all of a sudden things in the pants department start doing stuff all by themselves.

> Like what? Practicing the piano, taking out the garbage, doing my Chemistry homework—now, that would be useful!

You can be waiting for the bus or standing in the lunch line and all of a sudden...

HELLO!

> Well, hello to you, too!

And as for first thing in the morning, well, not all guys join the Scouts—but when they wake up, all guys can make a tent with their natural equipment and the bedspread.

> A what?...Oh, I get it!

We are talking **erections, HARD-ONS, boners.**

They come and go without any rhyme or reason at first. **But don't panic.**

Just because you get a hard-on in public doesn't mean that everyone can see it. Only Superman has X-ray vision. It might feel like it's sticking out like a flagpole, it might feel like you can't walk or like you've got an extra leg, but it isn't that noticeable.

So now that you've got this thing looking up at you at every turn, what are you going to do with it?

You want to explore it. You want to poke and prod it, to—let's be frank—masturbate.

Masturbation

Otherwise known as **jerking off, pulling the plowman, DOING THE FIVE-FINGER SHUFFLE,** *picking the pickle*, **SPANKING THE MONKEY,** self-service, and **CHoKiNG THE CHiCKEN**...to name a few.

Should we be talking about this?

Some people think masturbation is a dirty thing to do—but it isn't, and despite what you might have heard, everyone does it.

Everyone.

And you know what? There is nothing wrong with it. It's fun and it feels nice. Otherwise, people wouldn't be doing it in the first place.

So let's clear up a few of the stupid myths that surround masturbation:

- *It won't make you go crazy or blind.*
- *It won't make hair grow on your palms.*

- *It won't make your penis fall off.*
- *It won't give you zits.*
- *It won't make you infertile.*
- *It won't make you a pervert.*
- *It won't affect your ability to have sex in the future.*

I'm glad all this is true—otherwise I'd be in real trouble!

Now, for some people—especially those with strong religious beliefs—masturbation is considered wrong or a sin, which is fine if that's what they want to think, but always remember: **It's what YOU think and feel that matters.**

Never let anyone make you feel guilty for doing something that is perfectly natural.

Every sex expert agrees that masturbation is the best way to discover things about your body and how you like to be touched. It's a way of exploring and discovering things about yourself, and **there is absolutely nothing wrong with it.**

Whew!

Masturbating once, twice, even three times a month, a week, a day, an hour...that's all perfectly natural and perfectly fine.

And as a famous writer once said: *The good thing about masturbation is that you don't have to get dressed up for it.*

Masturbation

Okay, so it's normal. Everyone does it.

But what do you actually **do?**

Well, the dictionary definition of masturbation is "the stimulation of the genitals by oneself until one reaches a sexual climax."

Huh?

In plain English that means you touch and stroke your penis, usually back and forth and up and down, until a warm, tingly sensation starts building, and you begin to stroke faster and faster.

You might start thinking sexy thoughts about someone you're attracted to, your Geography teacher, or a favorite pop star. The **tingly sensation** grows and spreads around your body until it reaches a climax that almost hurts. But it's a nice type of hurt, like a big sneeze.

That's when you "come" and white sticky stuff, your semen, spurts out of the end of your penis. And **it feels really nice.**

That's masturbating. And one very, very important point: You never, ever run out of semen. You could masturbate every day, all day, for hours on end, and all you would end up with is a tired wrist and a sore penis. No guy has a limited supply of semen—your testicles make it on demand. Don't worry—you won't run out.

And it's not just masturbating that involves you, your best "friend," and a sticky mess.

You might also have...

Wet Dreams

What's a wet dream?

Well, it's a dream, usually—but not always—about sex that results in you having an orgasm in your sleep. You wake up in the morning and find a sticky spot on your sheets. There is nothing to be embarrassed about. Everyone has had one, and you couldn't stop yourself even if you wanted to, because your body is just doing what's natural.

Guys grow out of wet dreams—but no one ever grows out of masturbation. Ever.

Remember: If in doubt, trust to nature. Your body knows what it's doing, even if you don't.

SEXY THOUGHTS

While you're exploring your plumbing, you might be thinking about sex. That's fine, too—it's called **FAnTASIZInG**, and everyone does it.

Just because you might have sexy thoughts about your neighbor dressed as a large rabbit jumping up and down on a trampoline doesn't mean that you want it to happen. When you have these fantasies, you're just imagining things; you don't necessarily want them to actually happen.

You should **NEVER FEEL GUILTY** about what you think about when you masturbate. Whatever it is, it's normal—just don't expect it to come true.

Porn

Now, you might get a little tired of just *thinking* about sexy things and want to start *looking* at some sexy pictures instead. Pictures of girls. Or boys. Or both. Some with few or no clothes on. And if that's what you want, it isn't difficult to find. We are surrounded by pictures of beautiful people wearing next to nothing. Instagram, Facebook, the movies, TV—celebrities, movie stars, pop stars. It's HARD not to notice.

Hard. °snicker° I see what you did there...

You might start getting distracted by certain magazines every time you go to your local newsstand—fashion magazines that have girls dressed in see-through tops and standing around in nothing but their bikinis. And then you might notice the magazines on the top shelf. You know—the ones with titles like ***Voluptuous Vixens***, ***Sexy Singles***, and ***Big and Bouncy***.

Hey, that's my favorite!

You might even want to buy one, but most places won't sell a porn magazine to anyone under eighteen, so it could be a bit embarrassing if you try.

However, if you want to look at saucy pictures, you don't have to buy anything as old-fashioned as a magazine. You don't even have to leave your house. And that is all thanks to the Internet.

Just because you find yourself "accidentally" clicking on a link to GirlsInSeeThroughTops.com, it doesn't make you a pervert. Hundreds of thousands of men and even some women regularly enjoy pornography. After all, porn has been around for thousands of years.

If you think the contents of girlie websites are a bit shocking, you should see some ancient Roman mosaics and statues. *They* would make your eyes pop out.

And where can I see these mosaics?

But if you are surfing the more "clothes optional" corners of the Internet, there are some important things to remember.

Models in general, and models in pornography in particular, aren't average men and women.

They're probably taller and slimmer, and the women have bigger breasts and the men have bigger penises than anyone else you know. They are made to look glamorous, beautiful, and sexy.

So don't expect your real-life S.O. to measure up to someone on a website.

Or, come to think if it, don't expect the contents of your boxers to measure up to the men's.

Never forget that pornography isn't real—it's fantasy.

Don't feel guilty.

You're still going to be able to get it on with a real live person, and you won't turn into a rapist.

HOWEVER, a lot of people feel that any form of pornography is exploitation, and that the women in the magazines and films are being used and abused purely for the pleasure and gratification of men.

Whether you use pornography is a completely personal decision. If you think or feel that it's exploitation, and wrong, then there are no rules that say you have to use it. If you look at it and it makes you feel uncomfortable, or grossed out, or you think it's the least sexy thing you can think of...it DOESN'T mean you are any less of a man.

But what do you do if your mom has a quick peek at your Internet history?

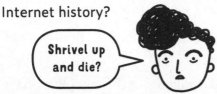

Shrivel up and die?

One thing is almost certain—she is not going to be happy. It might be that part of the fun of looking at porn is having to hide it from prying eyes. It makes it all the more exciting because it isn't allowed.

However, that doesn't change the fact that if it is finally found, the sparks will probably fly.

So what can you expect?

Well, everyone is different and everyone's parents are different. Some might **ignore it**, some might choose to **DISCONNECT THE WI-FI**, some will want to *talk about it*, and some will **GO BALLiSTiC**.

Not the WI-FI... Noooooooooo!!!

All these reactions, and any in between, are understandable. After all, you looked at porn over their Wi-Fi connection, and they might not like that.

It's always best to remember three things when it comes to moms (and/or dads—they might not be too pleased, either) and pictures of women with no clothes on:

No, really?

1. Your mom is a woman

(obviously your dad isn't...but we are going to

stick with moms here), and a lot of women find any form of pornography highly objectionable.

2. Your parents are older than you, and they might have different views about what is acceptable. What you feel is fine, they might find obscene.

3. Your parents may still think of you as their "little boy," and it might be a surprise that you are having sexual feelings now.

A Word of Warning

Looking at webpages full of naked beautiful women is easy. It's a lot easier than talking to a real girl, flirting with her, asking her out, and trying to form a long-term relationship with her.

When you use porn, there is no fear of rejection, no fear of being hurt—you just open the browser and you've got an instant two-dimensional girlfriend.

I prefer my girls to be flesh and blood! They are more squeezable!

But sometimes people completely replace real relationships and real girls with a fantasy relationship with the perfect woman from the Internet. Don't let it happen.

Your interests might be getting out of proportion if:

- *the keys on your laptop are getting stuck together*
- *or you find yourself more interested in spending every evening in your bedroom surfing the Web than going out with your friends.*

So? What's wrong with that?

Looking at the occasional porn site is natural and fine. Almost every guy has looked at something that could be described as porn at some point in his life.

YOU'RE NOT WEIRD BECAUSE YOU'VE JOINED THE CLUB.

But if it gets to the point where you have tons and tons of these images and videos hidden away, deep on your computer's hard drive, then you might want to talk to someone about why you prefer to look at nudie pictures rather than talk to real people.

I only read the articles!

Real people are much better.

They talk. They have opinions. And they laugh.

They're soft and cuddly, and you can go on dates with them. When was the last time you saw a guy taking his laptop for a hot date at McDonald's?

Well, actually, there is this one really weird guy....

Maybe you wouldn't feel comfortable talking to your mom or dad, but a brother or your doctor could help. It's okay to explore porn **WITHIN REASON,** and you're not a monster if you look at it sometimes, but always remember:

- *Pornography is not sex education. It's not real.*
- *It is not how men and women become intimate in the real world.*
- *It is not a great guide on how real people want to (or should) be treated.*

BODY HAIR

There is a whole avalanche of changes to your body when you go through puberty. And it may start with a smattering of BODY HAIR. But if you think you're going to go from *smoothly smooth* to a walking carpet in a matter of days, then you've got another think coming.

It's perfectly normal for body hair to develop at different times on different parts of your body, so if you've got hairy legs, don't expect to have a chest rug at the same time.

It's weird, but some guys really are hairier than others.

Like Bigfoot. Now, that's hairy!

But don't think that just because you've got a little bit more chest hair than another guy, it makes you more of a man—it doesn't.

And despite what you might have heard, it's not unusual to have hairs growing on your back and on your butt cheeks.

A hairy butt! Well, I guess it keeps you from getting cold!

Some girls make a big thing about not liking hairy backs and butts. But **DON'T WORRY ABOUT IT.** Unless you look in a mirror, you're not going to be able to see them, and if a girl gets to the stage where she sees your back or your butt, hopefully she'll have other things on her mind.

You'll also notice hair in that whole area below the belt. A mass of thick, wiry hairs, called pubic hair or pubes, starts to grow.

Again, no two guys are exactly the same, so if you're in the shower after football practice and you cast a quick eye around at the pride and joy of the varsity squad, you're going to see different sizes and shapes of penises and different amounts of pubic hair.

And by the way, you don't need to cut pubic hair. It reaches a certain length and then stops. You don't need to pop down to the local barber and ask for a bit off the top and a genital trim. But if you do shave your pubes, they *will* grow back. They're clever like that.

FACIAL HAIR

Facial hair will also start to grow, but not overnight. Don't expect to go to bed with no hair on your face and wake up the next day looking like Santa Claus.

At first, the hair will be soft and probably only on your upper lip and maybe on your chin. But over a couple of years, the hair will get thicker and more wiry, spreading all over your cheeks, chin, and upper lip.

As for when you should start to shave—well, that's up to you. However, it's probably best to wait until you have at least *something* there to shave off first. If you start to shave too early, you'll only irritate your skin and give yourself a nasty rash.

It's also entirely up to you whether you wet-shave using a razor and shaving cream, or dry-shave with an electric shaver.

Most guys start out wet-shaving because it's quicker and probably easier if you haven't got that much to shave off.

For Your First Shave You Will Need:

- **A little bit of facial hair.**

- **A razor.**

  A disposable one is fine, but one of the more expensive models with a swivel head will give you a more comfortable shave.

- **Shaving cream.**

  This usually comes in a can, although it is still possible to buy old-fashioned bars of shaving soap.

- **A mirror. Obviously.**
- **Hot water.**

- **Moisturizer.**

  If you don't have any, you could always use some of your mom's or your sister's, as long as you ask them first. Why not ask their advice? That way at least you get the right one and don't end up smelling of flowers.

My 5 favorite silly beards:

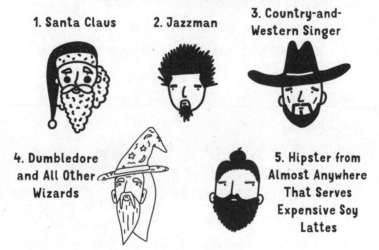

1. Santa Claus   2. Jazzman   3. Country-and-Western Singer

4. Dumbledore and All Other Wizards   5. Hipster from Almost Anywhere That Serves Expensive Soy Lattes

And How Do You Go About It?

1. Run some hot, but not scalding, water and wash your face with normal soap. This softens the hairs and makes them easier to cut.

2. Squirt a small amount of shaving cream into your hand, lather it up, and rub it into your beard. Or lack thereof. The idea with the

shaving cream is to reduce the friction between your face and the razor and to soften the hair even more.

3. Run your razor under some hot water and then begin to shave. Always shave downward, in the direction of the growth of the beard. Start with the cheeks and then work over to the upper lip, leaving the chin until last—that's where the toughest hairs grow. Rinse your razor often under running hot water, making sure that the blades aren't becoming clogged with hair.

4. Once you've finished, rinse off any remaining shaving cream with warm water and check for missed patches. If you've missed a spot, you can run the razor quickly over that particular patch again.

I'm as smooth as a baby's bottom (but less smelly).

5. When you're finished, rinse your face with cold water. This helps to close up the pores and seal the skin. Don't splash on tons of aftershave. Aftershave uses alcohol as its base, and that's why when you put it on after shaving, it stings. It's much better to pat your face dry, checking behind the ears for any stray foam, and then use a little moisturizer to give your face back its softness and flexibility. Using moisturizer

doesn't make you a wimp. It's very good for you and protects your skin.

6. After shaving, it's also best to rinse your *razor* thoroughly under very hot water, making sure you get rid of any clogged hairs.

7. You should probably change the head of your razor once every two or three shaves—leave it any longer than that and the blades will get dull and won't cut as well. They'll also become a breeding ground for germs and bacteria. Not nice.

> Eeeeww!

8. If you cut yourself while shaving, don't stick on a little bit of toilet paper. That will do nothing for you, and as soon as you take the paper off, you'll start to bleed again. It's better to let the skin close up on its own.

Now, if you suffer from particularly bad zits or acne, then shaving can be something of a **nightmare.**

> Ouch!

If it's just the occasional eruption, you can probably steer your razor around it, but if you are suffering from a really bad attack, you can try one of two things. Either:

Grow a beard.

(Which might not be allowed in some schools and can also make you look like you're a mountain man— fine if you are panning for gold in Alaska, less fine in New Jersey.)

Yee-haw!

Or: Use an electric razor.

Why? Well, if you dry-shave with an electric shaver, your skin won't be irritated by the use of shaving cream. A decent electric razor can be bought for about forty bucks and will be gentler on the skin.

If you want to try using one, it's probably best to go for a multiheaded razor with three small metal foils that make a triangle on the shaving face.

The other main type of electric razor has one single, long foil. This is fine, too, but the three-headed version gives you more control over a bumpy surface.

Just like with a wet razor, you have to clean the shaving heads after every shave to stop the buildup of hair, skin, and bacteria.

Which brings us to...

PIMPLES, ZITS, ERUPTIONS

(Otherwise known as acne.)

Almost everybody gets the occasional zit during puberty—but some people get them worse than others. What can you do?

Unfortunately, very little.

Zits are caused by pores in your skin becoming blocked by excess oils...that have been released because of the **hormone riot** going on in your body...that in turn has been caused by puberty.

And you don't just get them on your face. They can also appear on your back and shoulders and, to a lesser extent, on your chest.

So what can be done about these **PESKY RED, PUS-FILLED** monsters?

The most important thing is to wash regularly with an unscented soap.

You can try using a medicated soap, or one of the many anti-zit creams and applications that you can buy at the drugstore, but they probably won't do much good.

Normal soap and water are just as effective as any scientifically tested, new-and-improved breakthrough.

If your zits get particularly bad, you should see your doctor, who can prescribe medication to reduce the redness and swelling.

The two most important things to remember about zits are:

- *You should try to not feel depressed about them. They usually go away eventually and leave you with a smooth complexion.*
- *You shouldn't* **Scratch, PICK,** *or* POP *them. The temptation to squeeze those zits can be almost overwhelming. But don't. If you do, you might end up with scarring.*

GREASY HAIR

The same greasiness and excess oils that cause zits can also give you particularly greasy hair. Wash your hair often and thoroughly, and you should be able to keep the gloopiness down to a minimum.

Don't forget that during puberty, while your body is changing, your hormones will be in **FULL-ON PARTY MODE.**

How come I never get invited to hormone parties?

That's why you get zits and greasy hair.

And that's also why you will, to be frank, begin to smell.

BEING STINKY

It's perfectly normal—your glands are growing and changing, and for a while they will produce particularly strong-smelling sweat. It's nothing to be ashamed of, but it is a good idea to get under the shower or into a hot bath and have a good scrub down *regularly*.

> But girls like that manly smell!

You're going to get especially smelly under your arms and around your penis and scrotum and on your feet.

So wash them.

EvERy day.

And don't forget to change your shirt.

There is no point in getting yourself smelling sweet as a daisy only to put a stinky shirt back on.

Don't know how to clean a shirt?

It's very simple:

1. Put the shirt and some laundry detergent in the washing machine and turn it on.
2. Dry the shirt.

2a. Iron the shirt (optional).

3. Wear the clean shirt.

Notice that at no point in that list do you find the words *Wait for Mom, Dad, or anyone else to wash the shirt for you.*

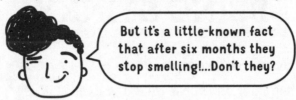

But it's a little-known fact that after six months they stop smelling!...Don't they?

There is nothing worse than body odor, or **BO**, but sometimes it just can't be helped. All you can do is shower or bathe every day and use a good, strong deodorant. Whether you use a stick, roll-on, or spray deodorant is up to you.

Stinky sneakers? You can get insoles that go in your shoes to cut down on the smell, but the best solution is to change your socks and wash your feet.

You can also use an aftershave and splash it all over your body to help hide any smells. A quick splash on your chest, after you've had a good wash with plenty of hot water and soap, will cover up a multitude of nasty aromas that might develop. But too much and you'll be walking around in a permanent choking cloud of perfume, which is just as bad.

Aftershave isn't a substitute for washing, and remember that a little goes a loooooooOOOOoooongg way.

So what about the other changes that happen to your body during puberty?

YOUR VOICE

How come you can be talking to someone and have a shrill voice one second and then, after a bit of a **WoBbLe,** a deep, booming voice the next?

It has to do with the Adam's apple, which is the part of your body that's just below your chin, sticks out a bit, and hurts like hell if you ever get punched on it.

Its job is to be in charge of the change in a guy's voice.

If you get a little excited when your voice first starts to break, it will all of a sudden sound like you've been sucking a helium balloon. This is nothing to worry about. It will settle down given a little time and find its natural, deeper pitch.

How **LONG** will it take?

Well, that's impossible to say. For some guys, your voice can take months to break completely; for others it can happen over a couple of weeks.

When puberty hits, your hormones will go a little crazy for a while, and that means your body might well get greasy, stinky, and spotty. Yay...go hormones! But it won't last forever. Invest in some kick-ass deodorant, wash, and don't let the occasional zit get you down. Because hormones have another crafty trick up their sleeve. Not content with messing with your body, they mess with your emotions, too.

CHAPTER THREE

SURVIVING TEENAGE UPS AND DOWNS

EMOTIONS

Guys have them. They might not like to think that they do—but they do. They feel **happy, sad,** *lonely,* **ANGRY,** BITTER, and *jealous* in the same way that everyone else does.

But the thing with guys is that often they just aren't very good at expressing all these emotions. It's all right for girls—they can get together with a few friends, watch a three-tissue movie, share some secrets, and have a cry and a hug.

Guys don't do that.

Can you imagine calling up your best friend and saying, "I feel so sad, I want to cry. Will you hug me?"

Ha-ha—who would ever say that??

It isn't going to happen.

Guys tend to bottle up their emotions, push them down, and try to ignore them.

Society as a whole teaches guys to be this way—to "stay in control" rather than "let it all out."

How many times have we been told to "man up" and that "boys don't cry"? Well, here's a news flash for you: Boys DO cry. Crying is good for you, crying is cool. Crying doesn't make you less of a guy...but it does make you more of a man. And want another reason why it's cool? Girls love guys who show they are in touch with their emotions.

Just because you're a guy, you don't have to squash your emotions into a tiny little box in the middle of your chest— they are NOTHING to be ashamed about. And guys need to find healthy outlets for their emotions. We need to understand our feelings in order to work through them. And the first step to understanding emotions is recognizing them.

Emotions. Show them. Share them. FEEL THEM.

WHAT IS DEPRESSION?

Depression can mean just feeling sad and low for a couple of days, or in more serious cases, it can be a medical condition that needs treatment with counseling and/or prescribed drugs.

How Can You Tell If You Are Depressed?

You might feel sad and listless, with little or no energy. The kinda thing you might expect from the phrase "feeling depressed." All very emo. But you might also feel really angry and aggressive and find yourself acting out, getting in trouble, and picking fights with everyone from your best friend to your mom.

You might think that there is **SIMPLY NO POINT** in doing anything—not getting out of bed or not going TO bed, not going to school, not hanging out with your friends, not taking a shower, not playing Xbox, not listening to music—and you might feel isolated and alone.

There is nothing wrong with feeling that way for a week or so—sometimes that's what being a teenager is like. But if those feelings go on longer, or if you feel down for a couple of weeks, happy for a couple of days, and then down again, it's probably worth seeing someone about it.

Sometimes, for some people, these feelings will become almost too much to bear. Life feels like being at the bottom of the ocean with no way of getting to the surface. Some people who feel like this might be tempted to hurt themselves with cuts or burns. It's called self-harming, and if you do it, or are tempted to do it, you should seek help from a friend, a family member, a school counselor, your doctor, or someone you trust, or one of the resources at the end of this book. No one needs to feel, or should feel, that unhappy. It will be okay—but the first step is asking for help.

Why Teenagers Have Ups and Downs

Anyone can become depressed, no matter what age. You can be seventy or seventeen and feel blue.

It's a myth that teenagers don't get depressed.

They do.

One in eight teenagers suffers from depression.

Many of them are guys.

Depression can be caused by almost anything, and often there seems to be no reason for it at all. A lot of teenagers get depressed because of:

Puberty (**Again!**)

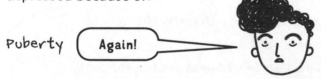

One of the main reasons that teenagers have **mood swings** and feel sad has to do with the hormone party that is puberty.

(**Well, at least someone is having a good time.**)

Puberty is a very unsettling time when your body goes through massive changes. Your hormones are at the center of it, wreaking havoc inside your body.

And they don't just affect you physically. They affect you emotionally, too, with the result that you can go from feeling fine to feeling like the sky is falling in a matter of minutes.

But hang in there, because although you can still get depressed after puberty, once your hormones begin to settle down, you should feel sad less often.

Other Reasons

Everybody is bound to get depressed if certain things happen. For instance:

- *Your girlfriend or boyfriend dumps you.*
- *You have confusing or conflicting feelings about your sexuality, gender identity, etc.*
- *Your parents split up.*
- *You have an argument with your best friend.*
- *You have to change schools.*
- *Someone close to you dies.*

These things are upsetting and always take time to understand and get over.

What to Do If You're Feeling Down

So what can you do if things aren't going so great?

If you're **sad,** you have to let it all out.

Bottle up your feelings and you'll become an emotional pressure cooker ready to explode in a big, nasty mess. According to doctors, if you bottle up emotions and deny them a release, you can make yourself physically ill. It's just not worth it. So how can you release them?

1. Cry

If you feel unhappy and you have a good cry, it doesn't make you less of a man. It doesn't make you a big sissy or somehow weak. Guys are allowed to be upset and vulnerable.

If you think being a real man is all about grinning and bearing it, you're wrong. Truly being a real man is about understanding your emotions and giving them free rein.

Been dumped? **Start crying.**

Failed that test you studied hard for? **Start crying.**

Your team lost the Super Bowl? **Start crying.**

That will always make me cry!

Someone close to you died? **Start crying.**

Just feel down in the dumps? **Start crying.**

I GUARANTEE IT'LL MAKE YOU FEEL BETTER.

2. Exercise

Sometimes, if you feel depressed, all you want to do is spend the whole day in bed or in your room with the curtains closed and **MOODY** music playing.

However, it's been proven that the best things for depression are plenty of exercise and a good diet. If you spend all day in bed because you feel sad, you are more likely to feel sadder, not happier.

Feel a little low?

Go run around the block a few times or shoot some hoops. **Or just go for a really long walk.**

You'll probably feel a lot better. Exercise is good for the mind and the body.

3. Talk

It's really tough to talk about your emotions, but it's the best thing to do if you're sad and can't seem to stop yourself from feeling that way. You might be surprised, but just the act of talking to someone about a problem—even if they don't say anything back to you—can often make you feel better. For one thing, putting words to your feelings can help you think the problem through.

Getting it off your chest, unloading, and then taking a deep breath and going on with the rest of your life will make you feel so much better.

Don't feel ready to talk to someone? Start by writing down how you feel in a journal. It doesn't have to be a great work of literature (you can even trash what you've written afterward if you're worried about it falling into the wrong hands—e.g., your little sister's). But often the simple act of writing something down can be hugely helpful in working out how you feel. It can help you start to put things into perspective. Even better, get a journaling app on your phone; then if you suddenly want to write something down because you're overcome with **FEELS,** you can jot it straight into your phone. It's also password protected, solving the problem of potentially prying little sisters.

4. See a Doctor

If your feelings of depression won't go away, it may be serious. Counseling and/or medication can help. A visit to a school counselor or psychiatrist will help determine if your depression is medically based and needs to be treated.

If you don't know where to go for help, see the resources section at the back of this book.

> Golden Rules of Depression:
> Never think you are alone.
> Talk to people.
> And no feelings, no matter how sad or desperate, last forever. It WILL get better.

Always remember:

- *Just because you're a guy doesn't mean you have to bury your feelings way down inside.*
- *Just because you're a guy doesn't mean you aren't allowed to feel sad and angry.*
- *Just because you're a guy doesn't mean you aren't allowed to cry, to break down and sob your heart out.*
- *Just because you're guy doesn't mean you aren't allowed to ask for help.*

CONFIDENCE

Confidence is **BELIEVING IN YOURSELF** enough to put your ideas out there, to stand up and make yourself heard, and to trust in what you want to do. It can be a tough thing to master.

Everyone goes through periods of not feeling confident, of doubting their abilities, or of just doubting themselves in general.

And unless you get on top of it, this lack of confidence can really ruin your life, because you'll find yourself missing out on so much.

Feeling:

> *shy,*
>
> *nervous around people,*
>
> *inadequate,*
>
> *insecure,*
>
> *or unimportant*

is a sign of a lack of confidence, and these feelings are more common than you might think.

Building Your Confidence

What can you do to build up your self-confidence?

You could start by making a list.

What if I can't write?

It's not dorky, it's not silly, and no one ever has to know.

On a piece of paper, write down a list of things about your personality that you might not like.

They could be:

> *I'm shy.*
>
> *I'm not very good at speaking in class.*
>
> *I get embarrassed.*
>
> *I blush a lot.*
>
> *I'm jealous of my older brother.*

Enough already!

You'll probably find it's pretty easy to come up with a long-ish list.

That's not unusual—most people find it easier to come up with a list of their bad qualities rather than their good ones.

Now, beside your list of things you don't like, write down the things about yourself that you *do* like, to cancel out the bad stuff.

Write down one **good** thing for every **BAD** thing that you've listed.

The good things might be:

> *I'm funny.*
>
> *I'm smart.*
>
> *I help other people.*
>
> *I'm kind to my family and friends.*

This list will probably be tougher. Coming up with a long list of good things about yourself can be a real challenge.

Don't worry. It doesn't mean that there aren't good things about you—it just means that you'll probably have to look harder and dig a little deeper. It is not the time to be modest!

If you're really having trouble coming up with enough, there is nothing wrong with asking your family what your good points are. You don't have to tell them that you're making a list—just ask them what they like about you, or think you do well.

So you've got two lists of qualities, one next to the other—some good,

some not so good.

Now get the biggest, thickest, blackest marker you can find and cross out each bad point, one at a time.

Really scrub them out.

Go at it like there's no tomorrow.

Get rid of them, so you can't see any of those things that you don't like about yourself.

Once you've done that, you will be left with a list of **good things.**

Positive things.

EXCELLENT THINGS about yourself.

I get it!

Fold up this list of your great qualities and put it in your pocket or in your wallet or store it on your phone. Every time you feel lacking in confidence, pull out the list and read through all your good points. For an added kick, find somewhere private and read the list out loud while looking in a mirror. Look yourself in the eye and tell yourself these amazing things about yourself. Why not try it every morning while you're brushing your teeth?

It might sound silly. It might sound weird.

BUT IT REALLY WORKS.

It's just a way of reminding yourself that you are a pretty cool person, even if you don't always feel that way.

Expressing Yourself

If you worry about expressing your ideas because you think that everyone will laugh, just take a second and think: "If someone else suggested this idea, would I laugh?"

If the answer is no, then why should anybody laugh at you if you make the same suggestion?

If you worry about public speaking: practice.

Sit up in your room, close the door, and talk to yourself.

Who, me?

Read out loud from the top stories on CNN.com. Say anything that you want.

Because what you'll be doing is getting used to the sound of your own voice.

Most people don't really know what they sound like when they talk loudly in a quiet room. You sound different, and it can be quite a surprise. If you've got a speech to make, an oral report to deliver, or an interview fast approaching, there is nothing wrong with practicing a bit ahead of time.

Have to deliver a speech to the rest of your class?

Read through it out loud a couple of times beforehand. Get used to hearing your own voice say those words. And slow down; when people read out loud, a combination of nerves and excitement means that they often babble really fast through what they have to say. Take a breath and SLOW DOWN.

Again, you might think this all sounds a bit weird, **BUT IT WORKS.**

Before you go into an interview or before you leave for a

party or before you stand up in class to give a report, there is nothing wrong with taking a deep breath and very quickly saying to yourself:

I'm great.

I'm good.

I'm pretty amazing.

I can do this.

I know what I'm talking about.

And everyone is going to be interested in what I have to say.

It will help to build your confidence at the moment you need it the most.

Body Language

Confidence isn't just about what you say with your voice. It's also about what you communicate with your body. Body language can express just as much as what you actually say.

Pop Quiz

If you're meeting someone important for the first time and you'll be expected to shake his or her hand, which of these is better?

(A) Stand up straight, with your shoulders back and your head held high. Grasp his or her hand firmly when you shake it and look him or her in the eye when you say hello.

(B) Shuffle in, slumped over and talking to the floor. Give him or her a limp handshake and mumble a hello aimed at his or her shoulder.

The answer is A, of course.

You can use positive body language at parties, too. Remember that you've been invited because you're interesting and someone wants you to be there.

When you talk to someone, look them in the eyes and listen to what they're saying, and you'll get along like a house on fire.

Here's a little secret. Ask someone what they find attractive in a guy, and they will list a few things: **SENSE OF HUMOR, nice butt**, and **CONFIDENCE**.

Stand-up comedians say that 95 percent of the trick to telling jokes, performing in front of a crowd, and being funny is confidence. If you are confident (or *seem to be* confident), people will pick up on that, and you'll be a big hit.

Have you heard the one about...

But what can you do if you get criticized even after practicing your confidence?

Coping with Criticism

If you do some homework and get a bad grade, if you tell a joke at lunchtime and no one laughs, or if you try to explain something and it comes out all wrong, your confidence can suffer a real setback.

No one likes being criticized. However, criticism can be very useful. It can help you improve your work and teach you when some actions are more appropriate than others.

Good criticism isn't about pulling apart something you've done—it's about highlighting strong points as well as weaknesses.

If someone criticizes you heavily, all you can do is walk away and think about it.

- *Ask yourself why the person is criticizing you.*
  Sometimes people use the chance to criticize to deliberately put someone down and make them feel bad. It could be that they are jealous of you or feel very **INSECURE** about themselves. It's a POWER GAME that some people like to play, and you're only letting them win if you let their criticism affect you.

You shouldn't.

However, bear in mind that someone might actually be trying to help you, in which case:

- *Ask yourself if the criticism is right.*

  A lot of criticism is based on opinion. Someone has disagreed with what you've said or done. If that person is important to you and you trust his or her judgment, then it might be worth thinking about whether the criticism is justified. If it is not, and you think what you've done is right and worthwhile, don't take any notice of him or her.

- *Ask yourself if the criticism is really criticism at all.*

  Sometimes you might be feeling paranoid and take something someone says as criticism, even when it isn't meant to be. Like what? Well, say your mom says, "Do you really like this music?" You might mistake that for criticism of your taste, when in fact it is only a question.

Paranoid? I'm not paranoid! It's the others—they're all out to get me— I know they are. Paranoid? Not me!

Whatever you want to say or do, you shouldn't ever let your own lack of confidence get in the way.

Practice,

take your time,

think about what you've got to do.

CONFIDENCE CAN BE LEARNED.

After all, we all have something to say. It is just a matter of finding our own voice.

Unfortunately, a lot of guys have trouble with a lack of confidence, and instead of reading brilliant books like this one to find out how to make themselves more confident, they depend on tricks to cover up their lack of confidence.

Which brings us neatly to the next chapter....

CHAPTER FOUR

SURVIVING TEENAGE SOCIAL LIFE

PEER PRESSURE

Is that like tire pressure?

When guys get together, they sometimes do silly things.

IT'S ALL PART OF BEING A GUY.

They egg one another on because they think they're being cool. They think whatever they are doing is going to impress the girls, or **THEY JUST WANT TO LOOK TOUGH.**

Here are some of the things guys do when they get together:

- *make mean jokes*
- *bully*
- *skip school*
- *drink*
- *take drugs*
- *fight*
- *brag about the number of girls they've been with*

You might think these things make you look cool in the eyes of your friends or girls, but instead, they almost always:

- *make you look stupid*

- *get you in trouble*
- *make you feel really ill*
- *do long-term damage to your body*

So is it worth it? **NO.**

Will guys still do them?

Probably.

Unfortunately, that's what guys can be like when they get together—kind of stupid.

But **you** don't have to be.

Saying "No"

It's difficult not to succumb to peer pressure. If everyone else is doing something, it's hard to say no.

You might think you're going to be called a *wuss*, **a dork,** or a **coward.** It takes a lot of courage and self-control to say no to your friends and to people to whom you want to seem cool.

You'd rather stay in with your girlfriend than go to the

movies with your friends? It can be difficult to say no, but if that's what you want to do, then you should say it.

You don't want to shoplift, even though all your friends are doing it, because you know it's **dumb**, *risky*, and **WRONG?** It takes real guts to walk away from them. But think about it this way: If these people really are your friends and you really don't want to do something, then they should respect that. If they don't, and they call you names, then they probably aren't such great friends.

This is particularly important to remember when it comes to things that can actually hurt you.

Always remember: Listen to your instinct. If you think something might be wrong—it's a pretty good bet it is.

FIGHTS

The way you act around other guys can be heavily influenced by what your friends think and do.

It feels good to be part of a gang or a clique, to be surrounded by your friends and to feel their support when you get into a difficult situation.

It has to do with safety: safety in numbers, safety in a group.

One for all and all for one.

Unfortunately, groups can have a downside. If you've ever gotten into a fight, you know that it's usually the people around the outside of the fight—often your friends—who are doing all the cheering and encouraging.

They're the ones who are trying to get the fight going, trying to make sure that the two people involved start slinging punches, which is odd—because if they were such good friends, they'd try to STOP you from getting hurt.

So why don't they?

Well, for a guy, it's still seen as an act of courage to get into a fight, to square up to someone and punch their lights out, or, if necessary, to take a few punches yourself.

But why?

Because that's what real guys do—isn't it? No? Oh...

What's the point?

Usually if two people get into a fight, it's over something stupid and small. How many times have you heard someone say:

"He looked at me funny."

"I don't like his pants."

"He said something about my mother."

Are these good enough reasons to square up and get physical with someone?

Not really.

Fighting

No one who gets into a fight really wants to be there.

Who would?

You might get hurt, and no matter how tough you might like to think you are, no one wants to go to school on Monday morning with a black eye.

You can't flirt with a black eye!

After a fight, the crazy thing is that if you ask these guys—who were going at it tooth and nail just a couple of minutes earlier—what all the big fuss was about, they probably won't be able to tell you.

Why?

Because the fight became more important than the initial argument.

But worse than you getting hurt, you could end up in a lot of trouble. It's hard to ignore a bloody nose or bruised knuckles. There will be repercussions if you get into a fight. You could get suspended from school, thrown off your favorite sports team, even grounded for six months. And that's if you're lucky, because fights aren't like in the movies—you can't break a chair over someone and have them get up, dust themselves off, and walk away. In reality, you land a nasty punch on a guy's chin, he goes down cold and smacks the back of his head on the ground, and the result could be severe brain damage or even death. It's called "one-punch homicide." You end up in BIG trouble with the law, possibly in jail, and the guy you punched...well...it's not a good ending for him either.

So why don't you just laugh off the fight, maybe shoot a few angry glances at the other guy, and walk away?

It's not that easy—sometimes you just want to sling a fist!

Because once you've gotten into that situation, where a fight might be in the air, your so-called friends tend to start egging you on.

"Did you hear what he just said about your mother?"

Who said something about my mom?

"Are you going to let him get away with that?"

"I wouldn't."

"Go on, let him have it."

"What are you afraid of?"

"I'd punch his lights out."

"You can take him anytime."

Sound familiar?

It's almost as if you don't have a say in the matter, isn't it?

But you do.

You don't have to do anything that you don't want to do. Even if your friends are encouraging you to start a fight, you can *always* walk away.

In fact, it takes more courage to walk away from a fight than it does to start one.

But what if someone squares up to you and decides that *he* wants to have a fight?

Surely then you don't have any choice—it's a matter of self-defense, right? Well, yes and no.

If another guy starts **getting aggressive**, getting in your face, **POKING YOUR SHOULDER**, and generally **ASKING FOR IT**, you might think that's justification for making the first move. You could catch him off guard and land him one on the chin. But then you haven't achieved anything. You've just gotten yourself into a fight that you didn't want in the first place, and now, because you made the first move, you have to finish it.

So what can you do instead?

TURN AROUND and WALK away.

The guy who's picking a fight with you will probably do everything he possibly can to provoke you. He'll call you a coward, he'll try to start getting physical with you, and he might even punch you.

But just like slow dancing and making love, fighting takes two people to make it work.

If you simply refuse to get into a fight, the fight won't happen.

Don't say a word,
don't get into name-calling,
or a shouting match,
don't rise to the bait—
just pick your stuff up
and walk away.

That's quite a tough-guy thing to do!

To be able to walk away from a fight, you have to be strong.

You might feel like a coward.

You might feel like a chicken.

And you might feel that you're running away.

But you're not.

It takes **huge amounts of courage** to walk away from a confrontation even though you know you might get more respect from your friends and more short-term glory from getting into a fight.

It's a bit of a cliché from old Westerns, but the guy who refuses to fight—even if he gets punched a couple of times, even if his ego gets bruised or he gets a black eye—is still the winner.

THE INTERNET AND SOCIAL MEDIA

Most of us live a large part of our lives online.

My gran's cat has a Facebook account.

It's already been said, but it probably can't be said enough: Once something goes onto the Internet, it's really hard to get rid of it.

Increasingly, as part of the vetting process for college entrance and jobs, human resource and admissions offices do extensive searches for candidates' social media and Internet footprints. That picture of you drunk? That angry or mean comment on someone's Facebook page that could be considered bullying? Even a review of a product on eBay or of music on iTunes...you better be ready to explain it when it comes to interview time.

I will defend my love of Bavarian oompah-band music until the day I die!

Your buddies might think it's funny to post pictures of everyone hanging out and drinking, acting like idiots, all over Instagram and Facebook, but it's going to be a lot less funny when a potential university or employer does a search and the first thing they see is your drunken butt.

My butt is never funny. Drunken or not.

Even apps like Snapchat, which supposedly get rid of the pictures you send or that are sent to you, aren't foolproof. It's all too easy for someone to take a screen grab, and then the Snapchat picture that was only meant to be around for ten seconds can be pinged all over the Internet.

So think about how much information you leave scattered around the Web, the opinions you voice, and the name you choose to leave them under. If your name is John West and you were born in 2005, it's probably best if your username isn't always JohnWest05 or JWest05 or John_West_2005. It kinda makes whatever you say and do online easy to find.

Why not go with Raiders_Fan_99, or just make something up instead?

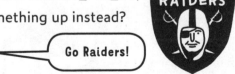

Go Raiders!

But a slight word of warning—very soon it might not matter what you call yourself online because face-recognition software is getting smarter and smarter and easier and easier to use. You can call yourself Donald Duck in every single picture, post, and comment, but if there is a picture of your face anywhere on the Internet, you can be identified—maybe even just before you go into that all-important admissions meeting at Harvard. And if that is the case, you are gonna want that picture to NOT be one where you are half naked or throwing up in the gutter.

You need to make sure that wherever and whenever you are mentioned, are tagged, or leave your identity online—it's the identity you want.

I want to be 180 pounds, 6 feet 1, and ripped. Can I have that identity, please?

I also hear @TGSG_RealDeal is a great account on Twitter. Apparently.

BULLYING

Bullying isn't just something that happens at elementary schools with little kids stealing each other's lunch money. It can even happen online, where it's called "cyber-bullying," and trolls (aka bullies) do everything from leaving horrible comments on your Insta posts to sending you malicious messages.

It's a problem that happens throughout life and can cause misery for the person who is being bullied.

But what is bullying?

It's using hurtful words to undermine, attack, intimidate, and belittle another person to their face, online, or even by gossiping about them to your or their friends. Don't ever underestimate how powerful words can be. You know that old saying "Sticks and stones may break my bones, but words can never hurt me"? Well, it's not true—words can be some of the most hurtful things there are.

Basically, bullying boils down to picking on someone because they are different from you or your friends:

- *It might be because he is smarter than you.*
   Or not as smart.
- *It might be because she doesn't have as many friends.*
   Or has more friends.
- *It might be because he has a disability. Or is zitty.*
   Or dresses differently.
- *It might be because she is of a different racial or ethnic background.*
   In which case it's called racism.

> • *It might be because he is gay or transgender.*
> *In which case it's called homophobia or*
> *transphobia.*

It can be for any reason—but whatever the reason is, there is absolutely **no excuse for being a bully.**

Bullying is based on ignorance and fear, it's based on stupidity and prejudice, and it's based on the "that person is different from me and my friends; he must be weird" syndrome.

If You're a Bully

So how do you stop yourself from bullying or becoming a bully?

There is one very simple way.

Next time you and your friends are teasing someone, calling him names, or generally making his life less than pleasant—**JUST STOP.**

Stop and think how you would feel if it was you or your best friend or your brother being picked on, being made to feel like you didn't belong, like you were a freak. Just stop and think how isolated and scared you might feel, how alone and desperate.

Stop bullying someone, stop making his life miserable, and give him back his self-respect. You had no right to take it away from him in the first place.

Bullying

Here's a question: What's the difference between bullying someone and teasing them?

Answer: Absolutely nothing, if every time you see someone, you tease them.

No one minds being ribbed or being the butt of a joke from time to time, but if you are always making someone the punch line of a gag, you are being a bully.

It's strange, but sometimes bullies don't realize they are bullying someone—they think they're having fun and the only reason their victim is getting upset is because he doesn't have a sense of humor.

But they're wrong.

Being Bullied

Unfortunately, it's not as simple to deal with *being* bullied. If someone is bullying you, it can make your life hell:

- *You don't want to get up in the morning.*
- *You don't want to go to school.*
- *You don't want to go out.*
- *You feel worthless, isolated, and weird.*
- *You begin to believe the bully's chants. If you get called Stinky enough times, you will begin to believe that you smell, even when you don't.*

So what can you do if you are being bullied?

Well, you could try verbally or physically standing up to the bully—but, honestly, that rarely works. The bully is probably either part of a group and has safety in numbers or, like most bullies, he's been clever enough to pick on you only when he knows you can't fight back.

A better tactic is to talk to someone about it. Your mom and dad, a teacher, a coach, or a youth group leader—anyone older than the bully who is in a position of authority and can do something to stop their behavior.

Or talk to your friends.

Never think that just because you're telling someone else about the fact that you are being bullied, it somehow makes you a wimp or a coward. It's almost impossible to deal with the situation yourself.

Bullies are smart: They often pick only on people who can't retaliate, either because the bully is much older or because the bully holds a position of power over them.

But really, bullies are picking on you only because they feel insecure about themselves.

Bullies are the cowards and deserve no respect.

It's not your fault that someone is bullying you.

YOU DON'T HAVE THE PROBLEM—THEY DO.

The bully is the one who is being antisocial and cruel.

It's easy to say—though much less easy to do—but don't ever let a bully win. Being bullied can be the worst feeling in the world; it can make you feel alone and desperate and so very sad. But you aren't alone, and people will help. The most powerful weapon you have to defeat a bully is your voice. Use it. Be heard, talk to people, and ask for help, and things will start to get better.

SUBSTANCES THAT MAKE YOU FEEL GREAT... OR NOT SO GREAT

It's not just how we act that can be affected when that ol' peer pressure starts swirling around as we hang with the guys.

It can also be what we do with our free time.

You could be having a good time, joking with your friends, when someone sneaks out a forty and starts passing it around. Whatcha gonna do? Everyone else is taking a slug, and before you know it, even though you probably don't want to, you're taking a drink.

Twenty minutes later you might be puking in the bushes—but hey, at least you looked cool in front of your friends.

Is that sarcasm? I think that is sarcasm!

It's a fact of life—you get a bunch of guys together and they will egg one another on to drink, smoke, try whatever's going around. So it's best to be armed with a few facts.

Booze

You might think that if you have a drink at a party, you will automatically seem more *charming*, **ATTRACTIVE**, and funny to all the girls in the room. You won't.

> If I became any more charming, attractive, or funny, I'd have to carry a government health warning.

Sooner or later, you'll end up passed out in the bathroom with vomit all over your shirt and feeling like death warmed over. And then, after you've stumbled home, probably thrown up at least once more on the way, and gone straight to bed, there's the next morning.

YOU WAKE UP FEELING AWFUL.

YOUR HEAD HURTS.

Your stomach hurts.

Your arms and legs hurt.

EVERYTHING hurts.

> Sounds like fun...?

And then you remember what you did:

- *You remember trying to put your hand up the shirt of that really cute girl from your Math class.*

- *You remember crushing beer cans with your head.*
- *You remember streaking across the yard.*

You look in the mirror and say to yourself, "I'll never drink again."

Why? Why do we put ourselves through it?

Again, it mainly comes down to peer pressure.

If all your friends are drinking, then it must be something that real guys do.

Booze Uh-oh.

First of all, it's illegal to buy or consume alcohol if you're under twenty-one, so drinking shouldn't even be an issue to begin with. However, in the real world, things usually aren't that cut-and-dried. Teenagers have parties, and more often than not, they've found a way to have alcohol there.

But that doesn't change the fact that teenage drinking is against the law and can carry some hefty consequences. Possession of alcohol as a minor could get you detained in a juvenile detention center, and probation. But that's not even the worst-case scenario. Eight young people die each day in alcohol-related car accidents. In fact, more than 40 percent of all sixteen- to twenty-year-old deaths result from car crashes, and about half of those accidents are alcohol-related. Is it all really worth it for a few hours of "fun"?

So what's a guy to do? You don't want to miss out on all the parties (especially since that cute Math classmate is sure to be there), but if you do go, chances are there'll be people drinking, as well as the pressure to join in.

Is it only a choice of too much or nothing at all when it comes to booze? Well, legal issues aside, no. It is possible to avoid feeling left out of the party without getting wasted and acting like a jerk. The problem, though, is that **alcohol affects your brain.**

It relaxes you, makes you feel more free and easy.

It gives you self-confidence—

it makes you feel funny and popular.

It makes you burp, too.

It also affects your judgment, so the more you drink, the less likely you are to be able to judge when you've had enough. Which means you're likely to drink more, because you think you can handle it. Which will affect your judgment. Which means you're likely to drink more, because you think you can handle it. Which will affect your judgment. Which means you're likely to drink more, because you think you can handle it. Which will affect your judgment. Which means you're likely to drink more, because you think you can handle it. Which will affect your judgment. Which means you're likely to drink more, because you think you can handle it. Which will affect your judgment...

And so on and so on and before you know it you'll find yourself slap-bang in the middle of that whole passed-out, covered-in-vomit, feeling-like-death scenario.

But surely booze isn't such a bad thing if it makes it easier for you to talk to people and makes you feel more relaxed or makes you funnier?

Not true.

The weird thing about booze is that it makes you *think* you are being **FUNNY**, *charming*, and **POPULAR,** but you probably aren't. You're probably just being **LOUD**, **NOISY**, and *obnoxious*.

Alcohol doesn't change the people we are inside.

Alcohol is not a magic potion that will turn an unhappy and insecure person into a happy and popular one. In fact, people are affected by alcohol in different ways. Some people just become very giggly and a little silly. Others become angry and aggressive.

And never forget that if you drink excessively, you are setting yourself up for all kinds of problems.

Like?

1. Hangovers

You have the fun—you pay the price.

HANGOVERS HURT: They make you feel awful for days after your drinking spree. They affect your ability to think straight and work properly. You feel *tired*, because when you're drunk, you don't sleep properly. Your stomach will feel awful and you might **THROW UP,** because alcohol in large quantities irritates the stomach lining, and your head will hurt because you, quite simply, starved your brain of water.

2. Alcohol Poisoning

If you drink too much booze at one time, you can also **POISON** yourself. The body processes alcohol by absorbing it into the bloodstream and then passing it through the body—that's how it gets to your brain and makes you feel tipsy. However, if you overload the bloodstream with more alcohol than it can handle, it reaches toxic levels. Then you might find yourself in the hospital having your stomach pumped. Not fun.

Don't forget about beer bellies!

3. Liver Damage

Drink too much for too many years, and you will set yourself up for a whole load of problems in later life. Liver damage, also known as cirrhosis, is an illness directly linked with drinking. The liver is the organ in the body that cleans the blood. It's your built-in filter. If you pass too much alcohol through it over a period of years, it will just pack up and stop working. And then you are in **REAL TROUBLE.**

This is all very cheerful!

4. Stroke

A stroke can be caused by a hemorrhage in your brain. Blood leaks out and shuts down areas of your brain, or fails to make it to important areas and **KILLS** sections of it off. Awful stuff. A stroke can leave you unable to move one or both your hands, talk, or walk. Although there are many possible causes for a stroke, studies have shown that if you regularly drink heavily, you are more likely to suffer from one.

5. Alcoholism

Some people can also become **AddictEd** to booze. They don't drink just because it tastes nice or they enjoy it. They drink because they have to, because they can't get up in the morning without a drink, they can't leave their house without a drink, they can't function without a drink. Alcoholism is a **very serious problem** that can lead to all kinds of dire medical conditions, depression, and death.

In most cases, alcoholism creeps up and overtakes you. That's why no one should ever get drunk because they think it solves a problem, makes life easier, or makes bad things go away. It doesn't. No matter what your worries or problems are, they will still be around after you have sobered up. In fact, given that too much booze makes most people act like idiots and gets you into all kinds of trouble, you may find you have MORE problems when you sober up, in addition to a hangover.

Get into the habit of drinking so much you throw up now, and you'll probably do it for many, many years to come.

There's nothing wrong with drinking in and of itself. Alcohol tastes okay. Drinking is social. Adults do it all the time. But...

There *is* something wrong with drinking so much that you pass out, throw up, or can't remember what you did while you were drunk.

There *is* something wrong with drinking because you can't face a problem or because you think when you are drunk you are a better or more popular person.

When it comes to drinking, always remember that moderation and self-control are the keys.

Cigarettes

They might not be illegal if you are over eighteen, but cigarettes can and do kill.

Smoking is a disgusting habit that only ever leads to bad and unpleasant side effects, from the purely cosmetic:

STAINED FINGERS,

smelly clothes,

poor skin, and

YELLOW TEETH,

to the terminal: heart disease, thrombosis (which is when blood forms clots and blockages, and that will give you all kinds of problems), and lung, throat, and mouth cancer. And while no cancer is a walk in the park, these three bad boys are particularly nasty.

Why do it?

Well, smoking relaxes some people, making them feel more sociable and at ease. And some teenagers think it's cool and rebellious.

It makes you look tough, doesn't it?

But why?

What is so cool about **smelling like an ashtray**, and what's so rebellious about COUGHING UP GREEN SLIME every morning?

Yuck!

Nothing.

It comes down to that old problem of peer pressure. Ironically, the first time you smoke a cigarette, it will taste disgusting. It might even make you throw up, but odds are you'll stand there with your friends, feeling awful, your eyes watering, and say something like, "Mmmm, smooth."

But of course it's not.

MMM—nice!...Someone pass me a bucket!

Unfortunately, smoking is highly addictive, and any of the temporary pleasures that you gain from having a cigarette are very quickly replaced by a craving for more and more.

Ask anyone who has been smoking for a number of years whether they would like to quit, and almost all will say yes. Ask them why they don't and more often than not they will say that they can't.

It's just best not to start.

Vaping

Also known as e-cigarettes. These are the weird gadgets that give out little puffs of white vapor. Millions of people have switched from cigarettes to e-cigarettes because they are considered less damaging to your health.

E-cigarettes come in all kinds of flavors, from what you might expect—tobacco—to what you might not—strawberries and cream. But whatever the flavor, there is still a big ol' whack of nicotine in each puff. Just like regular cigarettes, and just as addictive. Sounds crazy, right? While a lot of people think vaping is safer than smoking, the jury is still out as to whether it's **totally safe**, and some research is suggesting that there are *some* negative health effects associated with the use of e-cigarettes.

Also, just like with cigarettes, it may be illegal to vape if you are under eighteen.

Drugs

Man! We really are getting into the heavy stuff!

There are a lot of drugs out there, and if you go to clubs or parties or just hang out, it's more than likely that you will be offered some form of illegal drug.

If you're wondering what is meant by "illegal drugs," well, to name the most common: **ecstasy**, *cocaine*, marijuana (depending on which state you live in), *speed*, meth, **LSD**, and **HEROIN**.

Ultimately, no one but you can decide if you want to experiment with drugs.

However, all of the above drugs are illegal for a reason: They do varying degrees of harm to your body, and they impair your ability to make smart decisions.

Don't believe all the talk about some drugs making you happy all the time or giving you an insight into the meaning of life or being good for your soul. The truth, which should be written one hundred feet high in letters of fire, is that NOTHING GOOD EVER COMES FROM TAKING DRUGS. PERIOD.

They give you a quick pulse of pleasure and then can leave you feeling crappy for a long time. And, in the worst cases, they can leave you dead.

IS THAT A RISK YOU WANT TO TAKE?

So if you do get into a situation where you decide to experiment with drugs, just stop for a minute and think:

- *Are you being pushed into it by peer pressure?*
- *Are you doing it because all your friends are doing it?*
- *Or because you think it will make you look cool?*
- *Or because you think you have to because it's that type of party?*

- *Or because you don't think you'll have a good time unless you do?*
- *Or because you think it's fun to try anything once?*

None of these reasons is good enough.

So what's out there, and what are the risks?

Inhalants

When inhaled, certain glues, deodorants, and aerosols create a floating, empty feeling. These are not strictly drugs and not illegal to buy, but they can do serious damage to your lungs, heart, brain, liver, and kidneys that sometimes causes death. The biggest danger of inhaling any form of glue or gas is that it's very difficult to regulate how much you are taking in, so it's easy to overdose.

Marijuana
{aka weed, pot, hash, grass, ganja}

Using marijuana, which either comes in a resin or in herblike leaves, produces different effects on different people. It usually makes people feel relaxed, warm, and sociable, but it can also produce feelings of **ANXIETY**, *paranoia*, and paNiC.

Marijuana is far and away the most commonly used drug in America. Recreational marijuana is even legal in certain states, such as Colorado, Oregon, Alaska, and Nevada. And while some people advocate for its use to ease certain medical conditions, the long-term effects of marijuana aren't totally understood. It is thought that it can spark serious underlying mental health problems, slow your reflexes, and produce hallucinations. Is it okay to use because a lot of other people use it? Is it okay because it might be legal in your state? Well, that's up to you, but just because something is legal or popular doesn't mean it's good for you. Booze and cigarettes are legal—and we know the long-term health damage of using those. Marijuana? Exactly the same deal.

Synthetic Marijuana
{aka spice, black mamba, k2}

Synthetic marijuana has been created in a lab rather than grown. And it is a LOT worse for you. It's meaner and nastier, and is really best avoided. Just like "regular" marijuana, synthetic marijuana is smoked. It comes in little packets, some of which will even say **NOT FOR HUMAN CONSUMPTION** on them. (*I think that might be a hint....*) And that warning is there for a good reason—synthetic marijuana can lead to seizures, hallucinations, and convulsions, as well as deep and long-lasting mental health issues. And because synthetic marijuana is made illegally, the strength of what you're taking can vary widely. Have some, you might be okay...try it again from a different source and it could be ten or even one hundred times more potent, and that could land you in all kinds of trouble. Oh...and it's hugely addictive. In fact, you shouldn't even think of it as marijuana at all. It's nothing like the pot your hippie neighbor smokes while listening to Pink Floyd. (Who's Pink Floyd? Ask your dad.)

Legal Highs

We're not talking about getting a buzz from coffee or cigarettes and booze—which are legal if you're old enough—but instead from drugs that are made in a lab and can be picked up over the counter from "head shops" or on the Internet. It's a really unhelpful catchall term for almost anything that has a potentially harmful effect but is yet to be banned by the law.

Because these drugs aren't in any way regulated, you don't know what you're getting yourself into. Legal highs might be way stronger and way weirder than you're expecting. You also don't know how quickly they're going to affect you and how long they're going to last, which makes it frighteningly easy to overdose. Legal highs might not be illegal—but they can be **just as deadly** as illegal highs, and every year people lose their lives because they don't understand what they are taking.

Prescription Drugs
{aka opioids, stimulants, depressants}

Just because a drug comes from the pharmacy or your parents' medicine cabinet **DOES NOT** mean that it is safe to experiment with. In fact—quite the opposite. Increasingly, guys are playing around with prescription drugs to see what happens, and it isn't pretty. Uppers, downers, round & rounders...If you start popping prescription drugs like candy or knocking back cough medicine {aka syrup, purple drank, lean}, you are risking addiction and/or death. Leave them where they belong: in the medicine cabinet, to be taken as the doctor ordered.

Bath Salts
{aka psychoactive bath salts, Bloom, Cloud Nine, White Lightning, among others}

Not the kind your grandma has in her bathroom. This is another synthetic drug, sometimes called a "designer" drug, made totally in the lab. It looks like white powder, granules, or crystals...like bath salts, in fact. It is nasty stuff but ever more common. It is fiercely addictive and can cause headaches, heart palpitations, hallucinations, and paranoia. More frequent use can lead to heart attack and kidney and liver failure. Worse still, if you take it while drinking alcohol, the booze can react with the drug in your system and multiply its strength, leaving you in a real mess. Maybe even in the hospital. Or dead. Or both.

Ecstasy
{aka E, X, MDMA, molly}

Ecstasy is one of the major influences in clubbing and dance culture. Sometimes it's simply called E and comes in a small tablet, and other times it's called MDMA (or Molly) and is white powder or crystals.

It's associated with heightened perceptions and an overall feeling of warmth and happiness. However, the combination of ecstasy and overheated clubs can cause dehydration and heatstroke, and it's relatively common for people to collapse after taking ecstasy. As with a lot of drugs, no two doses are the same when it comes to strength. And because ecstasy can take up to thirty minutes to affect your system, it's all too easy to think "This isn't doing much" and take some more. Do that and you run the risk of flooding your system and overdosing.

Studies have indicated that ecstasy affects both the brain cells and the liver, causing long-term damage if the drug is used regularly. Also, after taking ecstasy, users often experience a period of depression and listlessness.

LSD
{aka acid}

LSD is similar to ecstasy in appearance. It's also a chemical-based drug that comes in small papery tablets.

Unlike ecstasy, it is a hallucinogen, which means that it can induce strange and disturbing visions. This is known as a **trip**. However, sometimes these trips can be extremely unpleasant and very scary—not unlike the worst and most believable **nightmare** you've ever had. And once your trip has started, you can't stop it until the drug has run its course. Prolonged use can lead to disturbing flashbacks that may occur years after taking the drug.

Speed
{aka billy, wiz, crank}

Speed, an amphetamine, is a powerful stimulant that increases the heart rate and body temperature while removing the need for food or sleep. And while it can make people feel alert, communicative, and talkative, it can also result in drastic mood swings, irritability, restlessness, and serious complications if you have even fairly minor underlying heart problems.

Cocaine
{aka coke, crack, charlie, snow, blow}

Cocaine is a white powdery substance that, when snorted into the nose or smoked, can boost feelings of excitement and confidence. However, regular use of cocaine creates major heart and digestive problems, as well as ruining your nose by eroding it from the inside until it collapses. It's also linked to paranoia, irritability, and aggression.

Cocaine and crack, a stronger form of cocaine, are highly addictive, and aside from the health risks, they can lead to both social and financial difficulties, as cocaine is very expensive and an addict will do anything to get more.

Heroin
{aka junk, horse, smack, dope}

Heroin is **FIERCELY ADDICTIVE.** It can be smoked, snorted, or injected directly into the bloodstream, and due to the sharing of dirty needles, it can contribute to the spread of HIV/AIDS and hepatitis C, which can result in liver failure. A temporary feeling of elation and extreme tranquility is rapidly replaced by a desperate craving for more heroin, as well as by cramps, fever, and paranoia. Heroin is a scary drug. People who get hooked on it—and it is REALLY easy to get hooked on it—lose everything. Friends, family, their health, and more often than not, their lives. You can overdose on heroin in the blink of an eye, and using it will quickly take your life to a dark place.

All forms of illegal drugs carry a heavy price for their use. If you're a minor, you can be detained in a juvenile detention center and put on probation. If you're seventeen, eighteen, or older, you can be sentenced to anywhere from two to ten years in prison for possession, and to anywhere from two and a half to twenty years for selling drugs.

But you don't only pay a legal price. The brief, pleasant sensations that drugs may create can leave you feeling like you want more of that quick high. Every time you use a drug, the downtime of depression, paranoia, and panic gets longer, and the good feelings get shorter. So it's not unusual to find yourself caught in a **DOWNWARD SPIRAL** of greater and greater use of more and more dangerous types of drugs.

Always remember: One of the great dangers of drug use is that you might not get exactly what you think you're getting, but rather an even more dangerous mixture. You're playing Russian roulette with your health, even your life, if you take something that a friend of a friend sells, or gives you at a party, or that you buy from a drug dealer you don't even know. No matter what they might say, you simply can't be sure of what they are giving you and the effect it's going to have.

And new drugs are appearing all the time, with weird names and effects. So just because a friend of your older brother says, "Try this...it's new...totally cool..." doesn't mean it's safe; it might not be.

It's also impossible to control your behavior under the influence of drugs and/or alcohol. You can end up making bad decisions, such as trying to drive a car while you're high, leading to serious injuries or even death for you and your friends. Is that really a price you're willing to pay? **THINK ABOUT IT**.

SO NOW WHAT?

Now...you get on with the rest of your life.

But always remember these **SEVEN** things:

1. Puberty is a roller-coaster ride. Sometimes the best policy is to just hang on and close your eyes. From shaving, to girls, to masturbating, to feeling depressed, to working out your sexuality, things can seem confusing. Almost overwhelming. But despite your body feeling like it's trying to sabotage you at every turn—it DOES know what's going on. Trust it.

> Roller-coaster rides make me blow chunks!

2. Keep in mind that once you become an adult, things don't necessarily get easier or simpler. You don't hit twenty and suddenly have all the answers. But the challenging experiences you go through during puberty will help prepare you for the rest of your life.

3. Remember, no matter what it might feel like, you are not alone. You don't have to face everything and solve all your problems by yourself. You have a voice. You can ask for help and still be a man. Every guy your age is going through the same things you are, and every adult male you know also went through them when he was younger. They made the same mistakes, were faced with the same choices, and went through many of the same experiences before coming out the other side.

   So don't be afraid to talk to friends, family, teachers, coaches, or counselors about any of the stuff you're feeling—chances are, they'll know just what you're talking about and will want to help.

4. Pick the **GOOD guys** to look up to, to admire, and to have as your role models. The guys who DON'T do drugs or get drunk every night. The guys who treat people with RESPECT. The guys who DON'T bully others because they are weaker, different, or less fortunate. The guys who know it IS cool to try to get good grades and do something amazing with their lives and not just let their minds turn to mush in front of

the Xbox. Let yourself aspire to something, aim high, have ambitions.

5. Don't ever believe the lie that big boys don't cry. It IS okay to be a man and to show your emotions. And it doesn't just have to be when you get kicked in the happy sack or when your team loses in the bottom of the fourth quarter. Don't be afraid of your feelings and emotions. Celebrate them, embrace them, enjoy them.

6. There is no one else exactly like you anywhere in the world. You are unique, you are special, and you are your own wonderful bag of contradictions and craziness. **It's cool to be YOU.** Don't ever be ashamed of who you are, what you feel, or who you love. Stand tall, stick your chest out, look the world square in the eye, and say, "This is who I am. If you don't like it? Deal."

7. Oh, I guess there is no number seven.

What a rip-off!

Life is complex and wonderful and scary and funny and challenging, and you WILL get things wrong, just as much as you

WILL get them right. And that's okay; that's all part of being who you are. Don't give yourself a hard time whenever you fail or screw up—a real man admits his mistakes, learns from them, and tries not to make them again.

Ultimately, **how you live your life is up to you.**

You are going to face a lot of choices, a lot of decisions about who you want to be, so don't sell yourself short.

Be the best man YOU can be.

It's really great to be a guy. Just remember...ask for help, don't be afraid, and always try to do what you KNOW is the right thing.

Do that, and I think it's going be OKAY.

Do that, and I think you've got this whole "being a guy" thing covered.

RESOURCES

HELP!
PLACES TO CALL, BOOKS TO READ, WEBSITES TO CHECK OUT

You've heard the quotation "No man is an island"? Well, that goes for teenage guys, too. It means that sometimes you can't go it alone. Sometimes you need additional support—**SOMEONE TO LEAN ON,** *a shoulder to cry on*, a person to **listen**, or some **MORE INFORMATION** before you make an important decision.

For starters, you can follow the official TGSG Twitter feed @TGSG_RealDeal.

And here is a list of organizations that might be able to offer even more help.

CHAPTER ONE
SURVIVING LOVE AND SEX

Centers for Disease Control and Prevention
National HIV & AIDS Hotlines
www.cdc.gov/hiv

1-800-CDC-INFO (232-4636) | 1-888-232-6348 TTY
(Available 8 AM–8 PM, Monday–Friday)
🐦 CDC HIV/AIDS @CDC_HIVAIDS
📘 facebook.com/cdchiv

Centers for Disease Control and Prevention Division of STD Prevention
www.cdc.gov/std
🐦 CDC STD @CDCSTD
📘 facebook.com/CDCSTD

GLAAD
www.glaad.org
🐦 GLAAD @glaad
📘 facebook.com/GLAAD
📷 glaad.tumblr.com
📷 instagram.com/glaad

It Gets Better Project
www.itgetsbetter.org
🐦 It Gets Better @ItGetsBetter
📘 facebook.com/itgetsbetterproject
▶ youtube.com/user/itgetsbetterproject
📷 itgetsbetterproject.tumblr.com
📷 instagram.com/itgetsbetter

LGBT National Help Center

www.glbthotline.org

help@LGBThotline.org

Hotline: 1-888-THE-GLNH (843-4564)

Youth Talkline: 1-800-246-PRIDE (7743)

🐦 GLBT Nat'l Help Center @glbtNatlHelpCtr

📘 facebook.com/GLBTNationalHelpCenter

▶ youtube.com/user/glbtnhc

🔳 glbt-hotline.tumblr.com

LoveIsRespect

www.loveisrespect.org

1-866-331-9474 | TTY: 1-866-331-8453 (Available 24/7)

🐦 loveisrespect @loveisrespect

📘 facebook.com/loveisrespectpage

▶ youtube.com/user/loveisrespect

🔳 loveisrespect.tumblr.com

📷 instagram.com/loveisrespectofficial

National Gay and Lesbian Task Force

www.thetaskforce.org

202-393-5177

🐦 The Task Force @TheTaskForce

📘 facebook.com/thetaskforce

▶ youtube.com/thetaskforce

📷 instagram.com/thetaskforce

PFLAG

www.pflag.org

info@pflag.org

202-467-8180

🐦 PFLAG National @PFLAG

f facebook.com/PFLAG

▶ youtube.com/user/pflagnational

📷 instagram.com/pflagnational

Planned Parenthood

www.plannedparenthood.org

1-800-230-7536

🐦 Planned Parenthood @PPFA

f facebook.com/PlannedParenthood

▶ youtube.com/user/plannedparenthood

t plannedparenthood.tumblr.com

📷 instagram.com/plannedparenthood

The Trevor Project

www.thetrevorproject.org

Trevor Hotline: 1-866-488-7386 (Available 24/7)

TrevorText: Text "Trevor" to 202-304-1200 (Available
3 PM–10 PM ET, Monday–Friday)

🐦 The Trevor Project @TrevorProject

f facebook.com/TheTrevorProject

▶ youtube.com/thetrevorproject

t thetrevorproject.tumblr.com

U.S. Department of Health and Human Services AIDSinfo

aidsinfo.nih.gov

contactus@aidsinfo.nih.gov

1-800-HIV-0440 (448-0440) | TTY 1-888-480-3739

(Available 1 PM–4 PM, Monday–Friday)

🐦 AIDSinfo @AIDSinfo

📘 facebook.com/AIDSinfo

CHAPTER TWO
SURVIVING ALL THE CHANGES IN YOUR BODY

The Boy's Body Book: Everything You Need for Growing up YOU!
by Kelli Dunham (Cider Mill Press)

Guy Stuff: The Body Book for Boys
by Cara Natterson (American Girl Publishing)

TeensHealth
http://kidshealth.org/en/teens

Young Men's Health
youngmenshealthsite.org

🐦 Young Men's Health @YoungMensHealth

📘 facebook.com/ymhealth

The "What's Happening to My Body?" Book for Boys
by Lynda Madaras with Area Madaras (William Morrow)

CHAPTER THREE
SURVIVING TEENAGE UPS AND DOWNS

Boys & Girls Clubs of America
www.bgca.org
info@BGCA.org
404-487-5700
🐦 Boys & Girls Clubs @BGCA_Clubs
📘 facebook.com/bgca.clubs
▶️ youtube.com/bgca
📷 instagram.com/bgca_clubs

IMAlive, an Online Crisis Network
www.imalive.org
www.hopeline.com
1-800-SUICIDE (784-2433) (Available 24/7)
1-800-442-HOPE (4673)
🐦 IMAlive Crisis Chat @_IMAlive
🐦 Hopeline @Hopeline
📘 facebook.com/IMAlive-155814097819999
▶️ youtube.com/user/IMAliveCrisisChat
📷 instagram.com/imalivechatline

National Center for Missing & Exploited Children

www.missingkids.com

1-800-THE-LOST (843-5678) (Available 24/7)

NCMEC @MissingKids

facebook.com/missingkids

youtube.com/missingkids

instagram.com/Missingkids

National Runaway Safeline

www.1800runaway.org

1-800-RUNAWAY (786-2929) (Available 24/7)

NRS @1800RUNAWAY

facebook.com/1800RUNAWAY

youtube.com/user/NRS1800RUNAWAY

nationalrunawaysafeline.tumblr.com

instagram.com/1800runaway

National Suicide Prevention Lifeline

suicidepreventionlifeline.org

www.crisischat.org/chat

1-800-273-TALK (8255) (Available 24/7)

The Lifeline @800273TALK

facebook.com/800273talk

youtube.com/user/800273TALK

youmatterlifeline.tumblr.com

S.A.F.E. Alternatives
selfinjury.com
1-800-DONTCUT (366-8288)
🐦 #Karen Conterio @theSAFEstore
📘 facebook.com/SAFE-Self-Abuse-Finally-Ends-ALTERNATIVES-100545512550

The Samaritans
samaritansnyc.org
212-673-3000 (Available 24/7)
🐦 Samaritans @SamaritansNYC

CHAPTER FOUR
SURVIVING TEENAGE SOCIAL LIFE

Alateen
al-anon.org/newcomers/teen-corner-alateen
wso@al-anon.org
757-563-1600
🐦 Alateen WSO @Alateen_WSO
📘 facebook.com/AlateenWSO
▶️ youtube.com/user/AlAnonFamilyGroupHQ
📷 instagram.com/alateen_wso

DanceSafe
dancesafe.org

DanceSafe @DanceSafe

facebook.com/like.dancesafe

youtube.com/user/dancesafeusa

Drug Abuse Resistance Education (D.A.R.E.)

www.dare.com

1-800-223-DARE (3273)

facebook.com/DAREINTERNATIONAL

National Association for Children of Addiction

www.nacoa.org

nacoa@nacoa.org

1-888-55-4COAS (554-2627)

301-468-0985

facebook.com/NACoAUSA

STOMP Out Bullying

www.stompoutbullying.org

STOMP Out Bullying @STOMPOutBullying

facebook.com/StompOutBullying

youtube.com/user/LoveOurChildrenUSA

instagram.com/theofficialstompoutbullying

Students Against Destructive Decisions (SADD)

www.sadd.org

info@sadd.org

SADD Nation @SADDnation

facebook.com/saddnation

youtube.com/user/SADDNational

Students Against Drugs and Alcohol (SADA)

www.sada.org

918-231-8313

Teens Against Bullying

pacerteensagainstbullying.org

facebook.com/PACERsNationalBullyingPreventionCenter

instagram.com/pacer_nbpc

Youth to Youth International

www.youthtoyouth.net

614-224-4506

y2yinfo@compdrug.org

Youth to Youth @Y2Y1982

facebook.com/youthtoyouthint

youtube.com/channel/UC2gGO23Mldbw1M2apqKJW9g

instagram.com/y2y1982

ACKNOWLEDGMENTS

Nineteen years is too long to leave between writing projects—there have been so many people who have helped in this major revision. Thank you, **Megan Tingley**, for remembering who I was when the email arrived suggesting I update the book. To **Pam Gruber**, editor extraordinaire, who has brought genuine insight and humor to this project, for at least pretending never to mind when I missed a deadline. To my agent **Laetitia Rutherford** at Watson Little, who not only offered intuitive words of encouragement, but also managed to sort out all kinds of issues—the next one will be easier! **Mum and Dad**—thank you for the years of love and support. **Stephen**, my brother, my best friend, and a man I will never stop looking up to. **Debbie**, my beautiful, loving wife, whose idea it was to revisit this project and who has had to put up with the lost weekends while I made it happen. Thank you, baby...nothing makes sense without you. **Millicent, Holden, and Genevieve**—the three little people who are my joy, my light, and my love. And finally, **Twiglet the Dog**, for the unconditional love only a sausage dog can give.

When not writing books, **Jeremy Daldry** makes television programs. As an award-winning director and producer, he has made shows for all the major British broadcasters, including the BBC, Channel 4, and ITV. He lives in North London with his wife, three children, two cats, and a sausage dog called Twiglet.